NINE LESSONS FOR BUSINESS SUCCESS

NINE LESSONS FOR BUSINESS SUCCESS

ALL YOU NEED TO KNOW TO OPERATE
A SUCCESSFUL BUSINESS

Neil Goldstein

DEDICATION

*Dedicated to my mother and all the women who have put up with me:
Mercedes, Arielle, Sarah, Michelle, Marcy.*

*Thanks to Cathy Harris for reading then entire book and sharing some
great comments.*
*Special thanks to Morgen Rich for her editing, patience, and guidance in mak-
ing this book a reality.*
*Special thanks to my son Dan who worked with me from the beginning when this
was just an idea.*
Special thanks to Brian Rathbone for his guidance and encouragement.

TABLE OF CONTENTS

Only too often business owners have ideas that seem like a good business to start, but are just ideas, not businesses. Those ideas are sometimes based upon unsound principles and have little chance of success. Financial projections associated with the project show great profits but are often cosmetically attractive more than financially sound. It is vital to examine the ideas and vet them for reasonableness. Avoid using statistics as the only base of reference whether from a governmental organization or your best friend. Gather as many facts (real facts) as you can before decisions.

This section will clearly illustrate what business owners need to focus on for the company, its employees, vendors, and ancillary staff. All too often, the owner starts a company and then does not want to get involved with mundane tasks like collecting outstanding accounts receivable or warehousing. Tasks like these are not as interesting as designing new lines or meeting with customers, but nevertheless, if not performed well, may causes difficulties and losses.

Companies generally fall into two categories when deciding on how much to charge for a product or service – 1) based upon the cost of the product/service or 2) matching the competitor's sale price. Either way it is essential for a company to know the real and true cost. Management needs to define what are "included" costs and how much in profits is necessary to cover expenses. For those companies limited by competition, knowing true costs will allow management to insure that overhead and other expenses do not exceed income. This chapter will insure a great education about including all costs.

It is unlikely any business owner can fully grasp how important having money is to the success of a business. A business has money in the bank, but it is the "custodian" of that money for a variety of others it will need to pay in the future. There might be money in the bank, but the rent is due in 2 weeks, payroll next week, and taxes next month. Is that money in the bank free to use to buy a new piece of equipment? This chapter will highlight how best to understand cash flow, cash requirements, and the pitfalls of spending money without a plan.

This chapter teaches how to issue credit and recognize good and bad credit risks. Look at many successful companies, and you will find a well-organized credit and collection department.

Bad management of collection also acts like a 2-ton anchor when trying to sail. Poorly done, the collections process can also hurt the company's ability to get new orders. Try arguing with a customer about collecting an old outstanding invoice and then asking them for a new order; tough to do. It can be done successfully but takes an understanding of respect and compassion. Collecting from a slow-paying customer is truly an art form few understand. Hard and threatening approaches can work, but following the advice in the expression "one gets more flies with honey" is the better way to go.

Most unsuccessful business owners blame their failure on the bank that stopped lending money and recalled the loan. A business can only operate if it has cash in the bank. Cash would be available if the company had profits or it had an outside source of cash, i.e. a bank loan, investors or the owner is willing to contribute his cash. Absence of profits the company must rely on those outside sources of money. Absence of profits how long will those outside sources continue to contribute money to a losing cause? Many of my clients recognized their failure to manage their bank loan too late and suffered greatly. Some even said their worst mistake in business was not understanding their banking relationship. Respect for all parties involved is generally the secret to success. Borrowing money represents an extreme weakness that others can exploit. Learn when and why to borrow money in this chapter.

Profits cannot be achieved until the paperwork is done. The more accurate and efficient the system, the greater chance of operating a successful business. Shipping orders seem like the easiest part of operating a business. What is there to do but pick the product, put it in the box and send it to the customer. Simple, right? Not so and those who have ever done this job know how truly difficult a task it can be without a great system in place. There are many possibilities for an error to occur after an order is taken. This type of failure is easily preventable by just following easy steps clearly identified in Lesson 8.

If any one category frustrates owners, lenders and staff, it's inventory. Inventory is like furniture in a house; it rarely moves and loses resale value each day. Companies spend money to purchase goods for resale. That which is not sold and remains in the warehouse is inventory; the key word being "unsold". It costs much to warehouse, finance, store and count during physical inventory taking. In most cases money was borrowed to pay for the goods and since they are left on the shelf, unsold, that money cannot be paid back. This chapter advises ways to sell inventory and recognize the detriment to company efforts.

The appendix includes a glossary, list of tables, and recommendations and suggestions for business owners, including what to work on during the week and rules to follow when operating the business.

INTRODUCTION

Consultants have credibility because they are not
dumb enough to work at your company.
— SCOTT ADAMS

Person 1 to Person 2: What do you do for a living?
Person 2: I'm a consultant.
Person 1: Me too! I'm out of work also.

My consulting business started because I was out of work. At 45 years old, it was not easy to get a job with adequate compensation to help two teenagers pay for college. My commitment to them and the need to raise my self-esteem were motivation enough to make a consulting career successful. Along the way, I learned a lot about how to help businesses succeed. Thus, I wrote this book for two audiences:

1. People like me who want successful careers as business consultants because they help business owners succeed in their businesses
2. Business owners who want successful businesses.

Starting my practice

With the help of some business friends, I began my practice with three clients who had a variety of problems bad enough for them to admit they could not solve them alone, and most importantly for me, who were willing to pay for the solutions. The tasks were easy ones, and success came quickly. Each day, I looked forward to work. It was mine! I would work 8-10 hours a day and felt guilty billing my clients because I was having so much fun. (I would bill about half of my hours worked to make sure the invoice was low enough for the client to pay without much review). The more clients I had, the more I could speak about my successes and promote myself as a "doctor" of business problems. It took about two years of diligent work to become fully booked with paying clients (I only use the word work for a better understanding of why I was paid. It really was fun and rewarding on many levels.).

My sales pitch was simple. I wanted work that no one else would take for a variety of reasons. Other consultants did not want my clients because they were new businesses, had low revenue, could not pay much, and were often difficult to work with. Not only did I learn much from this diverse group of clients, but also earned enough to support my family.

Although I had been a Chief Financial Officer, Vice-President of Finance, and President of successful companies, I knew little about why companies fail. With each new client I consulted, I learned a bit more about what led to failure. How could a business that was successful for a period of time fail? What prevented the successful company from continuing to be profitable? Over time, my experience revealed many of the issues troubling businesses were endemic. Having seen the same problems in different companies, I became an expert in recognizing business problems. As a result of focusing on the most common business problems, the success rate of my consulting practice soared, and it brought me a plethora of new clients, as well.

Over my more than twenty years as a business consultant, I've seen why businesses fail, and I've identified patterns in those failures. I've also identified nine critical areas of focus necessary for a successful business (or business recovery). To help consultants and business owners master performance in each of these areas, this book offers guidance in the form of analyzed case studies, worksheets, examples, and punch lists.

After reading this book, if you have any questions about your specific business problems or issues, please feel free to e-mail those questions:

Neilgbinc@gmail.com

Please include your contact information and any comments about the book.

EMPLOYEE OR CONSULTANT?

There is no shame in being out of work. Many employees get termination notices for reasons not related to their work performance. In fact, an employee's job security often parallels quite closely with the *ability of owners and management to succeed*. One can be an ideal employee and still lose a job because the company fails.

I have worked in both large and small companies and found both unsuitable to my style of working. In large companies, regardless of how hard I worked, the structure of compensation limited my ability to get raises. My managers often received instructions to limit staff raises to save the company money. My managers' performance reviews included how successful they were at keeping payroll costs down while retaining employees so that the company wouldn't need to spend money to hire and train new employees. (This was part of the nonsense I did not understand. Why not give the employees some of the money allocated for hiring/training expenses as an incentive to stay?)

In small companies, the owners took most of the profits for themselves. Each dollar they gave to an employee was one they did not get to keep. Good luck getting something from them if you're an employee. Often, if the company lost money, principals borrowed from their lender to take what they wanted, thereby burdening the company with more debt and increasing the failure rate. Employees are typically unaware of this detriment to the company's future and, therefore, surprised when the pink slip arrives.

How consulting differs from a job

Consulting is different from a job in many ways—from how one approaches an engagement to the urgency of achieving results. Despite the similarity of having to perform at a job and having to perform as a consultant, the rewards and punishments for success and failure differ greatly. Incentives, one of the great motivators in life, also vary from low at jobs to high as a consultant.

To illustrate this point, let's take an employed IT manager with the task of getting a new web site operational in 60 days. The IT manager's counterpart is an external consultant who is engaged to do the same job with the same completion time.

> *The Employee.* The employee works diligently with his team, working overtime, and completes the task on time. The roll-out looks great. At year end, the IT manager is looking for a raise. He boldly states how he worked and asks for a raise. The manager replies, "But that is why we pay you. That is how you earn your salary." How much of an incentive does the IT manager have to outperform expectations? The answer is little, as the compensation for doing so will probably not change, and if so, not by much. Moreover, what urgency does the IT manager have to complete the task? He would want to make sure it is perfect because if not he could suffer the consequences for a while at the company. Some manager might remind him of any errors made at the start of new projects.
>
> *The Consultant.* Management does not have an IT manager who can direct and complete setting up a new web site. Since the company has no need to hire a full-time IT manager, they hire a consultant to accomplish the job. The consultant receives higher compensation than an IT manager would get for the 60 -day period. (Imagine I repeated that last sentence). The

company benefits by paying less on an annual basis since they are only paying for 60 days of the consultant's time. (Did I mention overpaying)? The consultant also benefits by not having to beg for a raise. When the project is over, the consultant leaves for his next assignment. If something is wrong with his work, he returns and fixes the issue then, again, leaves the company's premises.

Very often, the consultant will return to the company to do additional work, getting paid additional money the employee had no chance of getting.

The consultant accomplishes the task in the 60 days, and the company's management is satisfied with the work. The incentive for the consultant to succeed is greater than for an employee. References are a large part of future business, and if the consultant succeeds, he can use the engagement on his list of happy clients and also may get a referral from satisfied company managers. Combine that with earning more than if employed at the company and you have part of the success formula. Add being one's own boss and time off without having to call up a boss and sound sick.

Completion incentive

1. What would the incentive be for the employee to complete the task early? Not much. The employee still has to come to work 40 hours per week. Whether it is working on project A or project B, it is still work.
2. The consultant could finish early and take a few days to either insure their work is correct or relax. (Usually those extra days are for getting new work, having meetings, attending business lunches, and networking). Additionally, the consultant usually gets paid upon completion making it of a greater urgency than for the employee, who receives regularly scheduled paychecks only.

The great leap

Becoming a consultant is a small step for man and a giant leap for independence. The risks are high, and the work at times is difficult to get. It is not for the weak-at-heart. It often takes years to get into the full swing to have a host of clients who pay. It also takes much time to acquire a list of people who can refer new business to you. It is similar to opening any new business, whether a restaurant or dry cleaners. The business of being a consultant takes time, patience, and hard work to succeed.

Should one make the change?

The loss of a job is sometimes a blessing in disguise. In the movie *Up in the Air*, George Clooney's character, Ryan Bingham, works for a company with the sole task of terminating employees in other companies (the business way, not the mafia definition). Management hires Ryan's company to avoid having to do the dirty work and reduce the risk of post-layoff lawsuits. In one case, Ryan asks J.K. Simmons' character, Bob, when he gave up on his dreams and took the job he is about to be fired from. Bob had dreams of being a chef but took the job to support his family. Ryan encourages Bob to pursue his dream of becoming a chef and to regain the respect of his kids. This scene was a bit dramatic but highlighted the point that pursuing dreams and a career might have some confluence.

After losing more than one job, I got to know the atmosphere just prior to firing. I wasn't invited to meetings, was left off of e-mail chains, noticed others looking at me strangely, and more. After enough of those comic scenes, it was time for me to try consulting. Hopefully, you're not reading this book because you're in a pre-firing environment but, instead, are exploring your options and considering some of the good reasons to become a consultant.

Good reasons to become a consultant

1. Each day working for a company is debilitating to your emotional health.

2. You can best utilize your talents working for companies that appreciate your work.

3. The money earned today is not equal to what you believe your talents are worth.

4. You are willing to work harder than at your present company and want the rewards, i.e. more time off to spend with family and doing hobbies, and the ability to govern over your life.

5. You have some money that will cover your expenses while you try to take control over not only your business life, but also your personal life.

Having no great illusions about my ability as an employee, I knew my terminations from companies were justified; I was not a good employee. I was that obnoxious employee always challenging the existing systems and protocol. Not every idea I had was good but thought communication and teamwork might lead to great improvement.

Qualities for success

After many years of pondering why I succeeded, it became clear three things were crucial, what I consider the CPR of consulting:

- **Curiosity**—to truly understand how things work and make improvements,
- **Passion**—to allow a full commitment to the profession despite having inadequately prepared clients,
- **Resourcefulness**—to develop creative business practices in order to succeed when standard business practices do not solve problems.

If you thought CPR stood for Cardio-Pulmonary Resuscitation, you were partially right—that comes when a business is about to file for bankruptcy and the consultant must resuscitate it to wellness (cash and profits).

And that's where the NINE LESSONS FOR BUSINESS SUCCESS come into play. They are the tools a consultant or business owner uses to perform CPR on a business.

- Lesson 1 – Have a Realistic Plan
- Lesson 2 – Get Involved
- Lesson 3 – Know Your Costs
- Lesson 4 – Money and Possession
- Lesson 5 – Credit
- Lesson 6 – Collection
- Lesson 7 – Understanding Banking and Bank Loans
- Lesson 8 – Shipping an Order
- Lesson 9 – Inventory
- Conclusions
- Appendix

LESSON 1

HAVE A REALISTIC PLAN

Failing to plan is planning to fail.
— ALAN LAKEIN

A good decision is based on knowledge and not on numbers.
— PLATO

What is a realistic plan?

I am not sure a plan is an adequate description for starting a business. Some plans, when verbalized, sound logical but in practice are far from reasonable.

Plans often fail for two reasons: unrealistic plans and bad luck or circumstances.

The most overused and abused plan (and one to avoid at all costs) involves statistics that sound reasonable but are ridiculous in practice. It starts out something like this.

I have a new medical device for the elderly that will allow them to walk better using a flexible cane. This cane absorbs shock more efficiently than do rigid ones. It works similar to the human knee and Achilles tendon, which absorb some of the shock when walking. A rigid cane also causes hand pain, as the person leans on it for support. The new cane has a full, soft handle that conforms to the human hand, allowing greater comfort. The cane will be manufactured in Asia, where the manufacturing costs are less expensive.

This is a good start to a business plan, but it's likely to fail because it veers into unreasonable expectations, such as those below:

> In 2012, the market for elderly medical devices was over $12 billion dollars (actual number from Transparency Market Research). If my company could capture a fraction of that market, it would make the company hugely successful. One one-hundredth of a percent (.0001) of the market would result in over $1 million dollars in sales.

What makes the above expectations unrealistic?

One cannot assume much when starting a business especially when it comes to market share. A company in business must earn its market share every day. Consider a restaurant that needs to earn return business as there are many places to eat. A dry cleaner, nail salon, auto repair and countless other businesses face the same issue of earning business (market share).

A new business faces additional problems of recognition. Who even knows the new business exists? Other existing businesses have already crossed the border of recognition and focus on market share. The new business must get over that first hurdle of customers knowing they exist.

Why are some business expectations unrealistic?

I would strongly suggest expectations are just prognostications about some future event, and who can do that with any assurances of accuracy? Without knowing the future, many business owners rely on the "experts" for advice. In the case of the Gelato store (see below), the owner relied on salespersons who were selling equipment. Of course, they would present a positive picture; they want to sell the equipment.

The correct way to begin a venture is to test the water by putting just one toe in at time. Use some resources and money to see if a product or idea works. If yes, put in additional resources and money to make it more successful. If not, change or abandon the effort.

Very important to the success of this philosophy is having reserves to continue a successful project, modify an existing one, or start a new one. So many of my clients ran out of money (the bank stopped lending in many cases as well) just at the time they thought success was imminent.

The birth of a new company with misguided efforts begins the process toward failure. The road to success is quite narrow, or many would be on that same road. Any time, money, or energy spent going in the wrong direction delays the company from achieving success. For example, consider a restaurant that wanted to cater to a healthy lifestyle serving salads, mostly of spinach. The target market is healthy eating consumers. The salads offered on the lunch menu are $ 12.95, a great value for the portion size and quality of the food. Few salads were sold because with a drink, tax, and tip, the lunch approached $20, more than consumers were willing to pay. The time it takes for the restaurant to readjust its menu to compensate for the consumer's desire to both eat healthy and pay less is their measure of success. The longer it takes, the greater the chance of failure.

Most unrealistic business plans race toward the end goal of how much money could be made if certain events occur. Some events are so difficult to achieve that it makes the business plan fail before it even starts. Here's an example:

> General Motors is a large corporation. I will show them my new windshield wiper that lasts 50% longer than conventional blades. They will test it and, after it vets out, will purchase 1 million units in the first year.

That sounds like a successful scenario, but it's highly implausible. When dealing with a large company like GM, it is important to realize their policies on new products are cumbersome and internal. They have engineers who have probably thought about this idea and even may have working prototypes in the system. Further a large company like GM doesn't ordinarily work with individuals, but known, trusted suppliers. A better way to begin might be to create a working prototype and try to sell the product to distributors who sell to auto supply stores. Of course, make sure any intellectual property rights (trademarks, etc) have been filed in a timely manner.

A realistic plan is important

A very important concept to understand is the difference between a business plan and an idea. Often a business plan has statistics followed by financial projections. The following case study illustrates why a business plan like this should not be taken seriously.

Case Study 1 – Gelato Store

A friend of mine liked Gelato ice cream and decided to open a store selling gelato plus coffee and cake (his wife and daughter were excellent bakers). He found a location, signed a 5-year lease, and began construction. The finished location had an Italian ambiance with café tables and stools, excellent lighting, and a comfortable atmosphere.

The owner's plan was to sell 100 cups of coffee each day, get catering jobs, and have lines of customers waiting to purchase gelato. He believed this would occur quickly.

Business was slow, so a chef was hired to cook lunches and dinners. Some advertising was done to attract customers. Again, no plan was offered to support these decisions except that they seemed like good ideas, and they were, but still few customers came.

The decision to serve lunches and dinners was more of an idea than a business plan.

What went wrong

If the idea was "stretched" and "vetted" out before any money for construction was spent, many detriments and adversities might have been recognized.

Here were some of the issues that made this a bad idea and a worse business:

- The strip mall was over 50% vacant, thereby suggesting fewer customers would come and/or maybe there was a landlord problem. (As an aside, it turned out both were true.)
- The minimum lease period was 5 years and personally guaranteed, making this idea very risky. If the business failed (which it did), the guarantor would be liable to pay the entire 5-year lease.
- Although not personally guaranteed, the equipment was leased and purchased making its disposal after the business closed a problem.
- The business plan did not consider a runway of time before it could become profitable. Imagine the business is an airplane taking off. It starts slowly, gains speed, and takes sufficient time to get to takeoff speed. The same is true of most new businesses.
- Due to delays and poor planning, the opening date was in winter, out of season for the product (gelato) in the northeast.

There are more reasons the business failed, but the previous reasons support the point I'm making that there is a significant and meaningful difference between a good idea and a realistic business plan.

The fix

Modify lease
Because the strip mall was over 50% vacant, a deal should have been made to secure a short-term lease. Sometimes a landlord will take more money for a short lease than a long one. Although it is more expensive, the risk is lower. On the shorter lease, an option could be arranged for the business to get a lower rate upon renewal. It is certainly less risky than guaranteeing 5 years of rent.

Minimize equipment leases

Lease only that equipment necessary to open and service customers. Add new equipment when more information is known about success or failure. Often sales personnel for equipment companies tell new customers how important it is to have all equipment on day one. It might be but not until more information is known about success or failure.

Target markets

The store was near to many schools—from public to Rutgers University—in New Brunswick. Advertising could have been done prior to opening, thereby gathering some interest in targeted markets. For the catering side of the business, few efforts were made to contact community groups like VFW halls, Lions Clubs, or Chambers of Commerce. Special offers could have been made to these organizations as inducements to try catering.

Optimize timing

The lease and construction should have been geared more towards an April or May opening, which would have been ideal for the product's consumption, thereby saving money in the cold months and establishing a customer base before start of the product's slow season.

What needs to be understood about business plans? Market needs

Commodity business

A business could be defined as a commodity when its product or service is available from many suppliers, i.e. pizza or a nail salon. Having a better pizza restaurant does not qualify it to be different, just better, maybe. The best plumbing service is still a commodity and in competition with many others.

These businesses should not have any great expectation of fast growth or great profits at the beginning. It takes time to establish a commodity business, often more than the pocket of the owner can support. A new restaurant first needs to be "discovered", attended and good enough for customers to remember and return for another meal. This takes time to achieve and patience by the owner. Using Groupon type coupons helps in the beginning but can have negative side effects, i.e. people maybe using Groupon coupons with no intent of ever paying the full fare.

Advertising in various local penny savers helps, but, again, not much should be expected from this type of advertising. Penny Saver type advertising usually involves discount coupons as well; nevertheless, getting a customer at least allows the business to have a chance at repeat business.

The plan for this type of business should be to have as many months of cash available for expenses and for the owners to pay their personal bills. Advertise where necessary and join networking and chambers of commerce groups to "get noticed".

And most importantly – be patient! It could take between 2 and 3 years to get fully established with enough business and make sufficient profits.

Specialty products or services

A business specializing in a specific service or product has both a more difficult time getting customers but an easier time closing a sale. If one is converting old 8mm film to DVD its customers will be less frequent than a dry cleaner but the closing sale is easier. There are fewer services like this than dry cleaners so it is less likely the customer will go to a competitor.

In this type of business, the same advertising is needed as in a commodity type business but greater profits are needed from each sale as there are fewer sales to make profits. The same advice for success is to join networking and other similar groups.

The plan might include having some form of back-up income to sustain the business during those times when few jobs are available. This allows less pressure on the business to produce profits to support personal needs.

Realistic goals

I can sooner kiss my elbow than have clients be realistic about their businesses. Clients generally fall into one of two categories; optimists or pessimists.

Optimists

The optimists always think positively and fail to recognize short-falls from their customers, employees and vendors. They always seem to be outraged that something did not go as planned. They have wonderful excuses about how they expected this or that and take little responsibility for the errors.

Pessimists

Pessimists are more conservative but fail to take advantage of business opportunities presented on silver platters, always believing something is tainted and will fail. They generally do not work well with others as their negativity is contagiously destructive to confidence and mental momentum, an essential part of success in most companies.

Optimists make up about 80% of my clients and pessimists the balance. Only one client in my 20 years of practice was right in the middle, and it was a true pleasure working with him. Thanks, Bill.

Realists are researchers

To have realistic goals, one must do research in various forms. A former boss gave me something to read on business failures. Among the many great points included in this article, one stood out as crucial to success: *most decisions are made using only 15% of the facts available.* Further, it claimed that up to 85% of facts are available, but people are generally too lazy to find and include them.

The concept is profoundly correct. For all of the years I have had to make decisions, this question was always in the forefront of my thinking: *are there more facts available to help me make this decision?*

An example of a client not using all the facts available to him included the following situation.

Case Study 2 – SP Elle

An apparel manufacturer (Sport-Elle) sold goods to TJ Maxx, Ross Stores, Marshalls, and other similar stores. There were 4 seasons in this business, spring, summer, fall and holiday. Retail stores asked that shipments for fall begin in late August and manufacturers to adhere to specific delivery dates or else suffer fines called "chargebacks". This required the company to accumulate all goods in its warehouse pending the first allowed shipping date for each store.

The company designed apparel and sought manufacturers in China who were lower in cost but reliable to complete orders on time. Different manufacturers were used, and completion of goods occurred at various times.

Starting in July, goods arrived at the Sport-Elle's warehouse and were stored until the fall shipping date arrived. Each week, more goods arrived until the warehouse was full. At the first shipping date, goods left the warehouse for the retail stores, creating room for more goods to arrive.

This happened for each season's shipments with fall being the largest volume, and summers and holidays the less important seasons for sales. The fall selling season was the largest because it included not only the need to purchase more expensive, heavier clothing but also the very large back-to-school consumer purchases.

When looking for new warehouse space, the client based the need using the fall season as the company's requirement for space. I recommended a study to determine how much space was needed for each season. The purpose was to take as little warehouse space as possible yet accommodate timely shipments to customers. Reasoning behind this approach was centered on saving hundreds of thousands of dollars.

The fall season (the largest) was from mid-July to the end August—about 6 weeks. During this short period, much space was needed, but at other times, about 46 weeks per year, much less space was required.

What went wrong

The client did not want to pay for the study to be done and decided to take a 5-year lease on 25,000 sq. feet of warehouse space, an amount that would accommodate the fall season's needs entirely. He paid $15.00 per sq. ft. As proud as a father whose son just hit a home run, he bragged about the great deal made, highlighting that all fall goods could fit in the warehouse. He used about 15% of the facts available to make this decision.

How much did this decision cost? Would $ 725,000 be a staggering amount to save by obtaining more information? Although the client did not pay for a study of his needs, I did one anyway.

The study found the most appropriate space required was just 15,000 sq. ft. This amount would accommodate 3 of the 4 season's needs (summer, holiday and spring). As this space was inadequate for the 6 week fall season's need, the plan was to have secure storage at another location close to the company's facility. The cost to store goods at another location, trucking to the company's warehouse, and additional insurance to protect against theft was calculated. The result would have been a large savings as follows:

	Lease Taken	Alternative Plan
Sq. ft. leased	25,000	15,000
Annual cost of lease at $15 per sq. ft.	$375,000	$225,000
Additional costs annually (trucking, insurance, etc.)		$5,000
Annual cost of plan	$375,000	$230,000
Annual savings		$145,000
Five-year savings		$725,000

Table 1. Comparative cost of warehouse space

The company could have used this money. It might have prevented them from going out of business.

The fix

One can only imagine how difficult it would be to fix a contractual problem like a lease. As a good consultant, one who never gives up, a suggestion was made to the client on a fix.

Because this business had extra space and available employees, who were not very busy for most of the year, it could have offered warehousing, packing, and shipping services. These companies are often called "Pick and Packs". A company that does not want to have their own warehouse expenses hires an independent company to receive, store, pick, pack and ship their goods. For most of the year, SP Elle could have done this. Another idea would be to lease some of the unused warehouse space to companies who are in need.

As it might be difficult to find companies who might need these type services, an attempt should be made to offset the extra expenses in the off season.

Additional unrealistic plans
Case Study 3 – AAA Books

AAA Books sold books online and to retail stores. The company had a bank loan to support the purchases of new books. Upon review of the loan, the lender noticed the loan only increased with few reductions during a year. The lender asked me to conduct a collateral audit—that is, a review of the company on behalf of the bank. This is standard with companies whose credit is somewhat suspect and allows the lender to gain confidence their loan is secure.

Don't be misled to think the bank paid for the audit. The bank may have paid my firm, but they charged the company an amount greater than my fee. Did you expect anything different?

A1's business was easy to understand. Half of the revenue was selling cheap, "remainder" type books to retailers across the country. Purchasing unsold books from publishers and selling to stores looking to offer customers a bargain on a book that once sold for much more was an easy plan to follow.

The other half of revenue was generated by selling directly to consumers through Amazon using its "secret weapon". The secret weapon was a bomb that exploded and destroyed company profits. Management wrote software to surf the Amazon site searching competitor's prices and automatically changing A1's prices to beat the competitors by 1 cent, thereby making it the lowest price. A1's books were always the cheapest and would appear first when an Amazon customer would search for that specific used book. Sales grew and grew until more people were hired just to keep up with the demand. The CFO and owner were especially excited about how well the "secret weapon" was working.

One need not be Sherlock Holmes to figure out A1 was inevitably going to fail.

What went wrong

A1 had no control over their profit. Revenue changed based on the whims of their competitors, but their costs were ever increasing.

Additional staff members were needed to handle the increased business. By "racing to the bottom" of the profit scale, the company made profits on each book but nowhere near the amount required to pay its bills. Among the expenses to be paid from gross profit were the costs of leasing a large warehouse and a continually growing number of employees to fill the orders. Additional equipment was obtained to automate the packing and shipping of books, yet another additional expense.

A1 was dead simply because gross profit was not sufficient to pay all expenses. The cause was a very bad plan that, unfortunately, was successful at putting them out of business.

AAA Books' aftermath

In trying not to close the doors or declare bankruptcy, a meeting was arranged for the approximately 20 publishers who sold books to A1. The plan was to present company changes that would give it a chance to survive in business. Publishers were going to be asked to wait a short period of time before getting paid while continuing to ship new product for cash payments (no additional credit). Without most publishers accepting the plan, the company could not continue in business. Everybody at that meeting had experience in the industry and knew what we were going to say prior to our presentation but came anyway, most likely out of respect and curiosity. We prepared a heart-warming story of humility and sorrow in which the owner gets redemption by paying off the suppliers and riding into the sunset with great profits. The owner rehearsed the day before the meeting, but he didn't believe the story himself and his acting ability was suspect. My role was to play Emilio Estevez in *The Mighty Ducks*, encouraging my client with words like "you can do it" or "believe in yourself". Unlike the Ducks, he did not succeed. Only Hollywood can pull that off with ease.

Remember Michael Clarke Duncan walking to his execution in front of Tom Hanks in *The Green Mile?* That was my client walking to the publishers meeting. He walked slowly towards the podium stage. Like the warden in movies, I felt the need hold him up as his knees seemed to buckle. All invitees attended the meeting bar none; it was a full house. My only worry was whether my client could hit the key points with crescendo and feeling.

The meeting couldn't have started better. We introduced everyone at the dais and explained the reason for the meeting. Nobody was surprise; after all, they hadn't been paid in a while. I turned the meeting over to my client. Head bowed, my client headed for the podium. He did not get to a few words before he welled up with emotion and couldn't continue. The dramatic pause was excruciating for everyone in the room. I took his place and continued the meeting, presenting the plan and answering questions. The plan introduced at the meeting had successfully worked in other companies, and the meeting went as well as it could have.

The company was not able to recover and was sold to a competitor.

The fix

Part 1 - Projections
First, projections needed to be completed to determine if profits could be made with this business philosophy. If yes, then it would be necessary to keep overhead down to the lowest amount possible. Staff members and warehousing space needed to be at a minimum. If projections show this model to be unprofitable, then it would be necessary to stop using the secret weapon and design new formats by which the company could make money.

Part 2 – Rapid response tools
A1 needed to recognize their unsuccessful actions more quickly. In most companies, daily reports, sometimes called "flash" reports, are used to monitor daily activity. If A1 had reviewed their profits and cash on a more frequent basis than monthly (their methodology), they would have witnessed the calamitous effect of their actions.

Why daily? Imagine that a company's financial system is reconciled every month. Business for the month of September is accumulated, and the results are completed by October 15. It seems like a legitimate way to do business, but that could be dangerous and lead into traps similar to the one AAA Books fell prey to. If something went wrong on September 1, it would take 45 days to discover.

In today's business world, companies need to be great, not just good; competition makes this so. Company internal systems should be set up so activities are checked periodically and, if effective, daily.

Case study 4 – HH Apparel

One of my favorite clients was Anna C, who often referred my services after I helped her company out of a jam. This lead was to HH Apparel, a lady's apparel and accessory company that had an online web site and a retail store in Brooklyn. They had grown to a few million dollars in sales, mostly from the online store. Despite a strong year of sales and profits, cash was tight and the company wasn't able to pay its suppliers for the upcoming season's new line.

When talking to a new client, I usually offer to work at no charge for a short amount of time. It helps me to determine if I can help and if so, how much to charge. In addition to helping get my foot in the door, it allows the potential client to see a true commitment on my part. After working for a couple of days at HH Apparel, I discovered the following three things:

1. The company designed a line of women's clothing and accessories.
2. It placed orders with manufacturers for a **fixed** number of products.
3. Most of the online sales occurred during one of four yearly sales. Many of their customers knew about the company's policy of offering deep discounts during one of these sales.

Let's review the three findings in detail to see why this philosophy is an unrealistic plan for a business.

What went wrong

1. The company designed a line of women's clothing and accessories.

With the fickle buying habits of the general public, it is quite hard to design an apparel line that would be pleasing and profitable every season. Nevertheless, this is the nature of the business, not only for HH but for many others. A plan of this nature is acceptable and widely used by many businesses, especially since HH had a loyal following of customer who purchased season after season. Number 1 seemed normal to me. No issue.

2. The company placed orders with manufacturers for a fixed number of products.

Number 2 was quite restrictive and most certainly reduced the possibility of the company having a run-away hit product that could cover any losses from other slower-selling garments. Here is where the plan began to go wrong. HH used suppliers in Asia who manufactured a specific number of goods. This, too, is normal in the industry, but HH failed to recognize that a good selling garment should have a life after the initial production run. If customers want to purchase product but cannot because it is not available, the company should try to find a way to make it available. One way would be to give a portion of the production to a local contractor who could make the garments locally, thereby allowing new orders to be filled for greater profits. Early in the selling process, good selling items could be recognized and plans to have a local contractor make more could begin. (There are other considerations in doing this—i.e., having the correct fabric available, but the concept is the important part to understand.)

One might suggest that customers who knew the limitations of available product would pay more to get a garment fearing they might not get it. This sounds good but is offset by number 3.

3. Most of the online sales occurred during one of four yearly sales. Many of HH's customers knew about the company's policy of offering deep discounts during one of these sales.

Having most of a company's sales occur during a sales period is almost as scary as ordering a fixed number of products for a season. The laws of business suggest at some stage of their existence, the business will have great difficulties because it is improbable to design lines of apparel that sell every season.

The loyal customer base knew the company's policy of having quarterly sales in which garments were marked down in price as much as 50%. The higher discounts were on garments that did not sell well, but all items were discounted, even the good-selling ones. Discounts surely helped the company dispose of poor-selling garments but at a cost: discounting good-selling garments that could have made higher profits.

Analysis showed that:

- The only garments remaining in inventory were the slower-selling items; price was not an issue for sales on these garments.
- Although sales were great during the sales times, the total amount of money received during a year was insufficient to cover expenses.
- After the sales period, new sales were almost non-existent, thereby creating an extreme need for cash or bank loans.

Was there a better plan for this company? I believed so and presented one.

The fix

HH had some positives that needed to be capitalized and promoted: a great product and customer base. But those positives were not enough to prevent them from losing money.

The recommendation was to change the structure of the sale process. Company policy was to keep items at the original price until the sale date when they would precipitously drop to the low sale price. The company's strategy was to take a bag that sold for $352 each day and immediately change the price to $200 on day 1 of the sale period. This dramatic drop was consistent from season to season, known by the customers, who, if patient, could save much money. The belief was the customer would make a purchase, but when?

My idea was to slowly drop the price each day of the sale period, allowing the customer to purchase at a price they felt the item was worth. The fear of not getting the item would hopefully prompt a customer to purchase sooner rather than later. If the company could engage the customer by offering lower prices each day, it might spark a sale before the lowest price was arrived at. It was like a competitive sale process in which a customer would have to purchase the product before another customer did because of the limited number of garments available. Customers would come to the website to see what the price was, but they would feel the need to purchase the bag before the price got so low that it was sold out.

The technical term for this is *capturing the consumer surplus*. Everybody is willing to pay a different amount for things. An artist may be willing to pay $2,000 for a powerful computer whereas a $300 laptop may be good enough for others. If a company only has one product that costs $2,000, then its only customer will be the artist. If the company only has a $300 product, the company will miss out on a $2,000 sale. That $1,700 difference between the $2,000 that the artist is willing to pay and the $300 that they did pay is the consumer surplus. That's $1,700 the consumer is willing to pay but the company won't receive. This is a contrived example, but it shows why companies should offer products at different price points.

By slowly dropping the price, HH Apparel could have captured the maximum price that every customer is willing to pay for their products. This might have made the difference that would have allowed the company to stay in business and make profits.

Example 1: All product sold at the discount price

Item	Quantity	Original Price	Sale Price	Amt Sold	Revenue	
Dress	50	$ 250.00	$ 150.00	50	$ 7,500.00	
Pant	75	$ 125.00	$ 65.00	75	$ 4,875.00	
Skirt	50	$ 90.00	$ 55.00	50	$ 2,750.00	
Scarf	50	$ 150.00	$ 105.00	50	$ 5,250.00	
				Total	$ 20,375.00	(a)

Example 2: A gradual reduction in the sale price
(For the sake of brevity, the example covers 3 days only)

Day 1 - Price decreased but not the lowest sale price

Item	Quantity	Original Price	Sale Price	Amt Sold	Revenue
Dress	50	$ 250.00	$ 195.00	10	$ 1,950.00
Pant	75	$ 125.00	$ 105.00	15	$ 1,575.00
Skirt	50	$ 90.00	$ 85.00	10	$ 850.00
Scarf	50	$ 150.00	$ 125.00	10	$ 1,250.00
				Total	$ 5,625.00

Day 2 - Price decreased again but not to the lowest price

Item	Quantity	Original Price	Sale Price	Amt Sold	Revenue
Dress	40	$ 250.00	$ 185.00	15	$ 2,775.00
Pant	60	$ 125.00	$ 100.00	20	$ 2,000.00
Skirt	40	$ 90.00	$ 80.00	15	$ 1,200.00
Scarf	40	$ 150.00	$ 120.00	15	$ 1,800.00
				Total	$ 7,775.00

Day 3 - Price brought down to the lowest sale price

Item	Quantity	Original Price	Sale Price	Amt Sold	Revenue
Dress	25	$ 250.00	$ 175.00	25	$ 4,375.00
Pant	40	$ 125.00	$ 95.00	40	$ 3,800.00
Skirt	25	$ 90.00	$ 75.00	25	$ 1,875.00
Scarf	25	$ 150.00	$ 115.00	25	$ 2,875.00
				Total	$ 12,925.00

Total of 3 sale days

Item	Quantity	Original Price	Sale Price	Amt Sold	Revenue	
Dress		$ 250.00		50	$ 9,100.00	
Pant		$ 125.00		75	$ 7,375.00	
Skirt		$ 90.00		50	$ 3,925.00	
Scarf		$ 150.00		50	$ 5,925.00	
				Total	$ 26,325.00	
Compare to total of example 1 - one drop in price					$ 20,375.00	(a)
		Additional money earned			$ 5,950.00	
					29%	

Table 2. Comparison of actual and projected methodology

Key terms

Commodity Business: A business that sells basic items or services like milk, dry cleaning, pizza.

Consumer surplus: The difference between the lowest price a customer has paid for a product and the highest price a customer would be willing to pay for that same product.

Measures of Success: Efforts of a business idea reviewed for accomplishments, i.e. money in the bank, new customers, competent staff. Each category can have its own measure of success.

Projections: A plan created prior to beginning a business to test the likelihood of success.

Seasonal Businesses: Businesses whose product is purchased more in one season than another, i.e. ice cream, heating and air conditioning, sun block.

Target Markets: Segment of the population identified as the most interested in purchasing goods or services from the company.

Lesson 1 Takeaways

SEEK ADVICE from trusted advisors BEFORE making what might be a fatal decision. It is usually true that many do not share the same vision, but one needs to listen to others to get insight into something unknown or not considered. Few students take the hardest classes and get 100% on all exams. Yet, take many smart students and allow them to collectively take the same exam, and the chances of getting an A grade increases significantly.

BE CONSERVATIVE. This does not mean to take a pessimistic view of the business but a realistic one. In projections, consider various scenarios that might take place. Doing so will help to understand remedies if the business is not meeting immediate goals. For example, assume it will take 3 months to find a location for a business. Then rework the projection using 6 months. This many not happen but will help to an-swer some questions should it occur.

Summary

- A long time ago, I heard about the "Scientific Method" of testing a theory. Before making important business decisions like start-ing a new business and materially changing an existing one, try the process below.
- DO NOT RUSH INTO DIFFICULT DECISIONS just because one wants to start a business or have a difficult decision resolved; time is often an enemy of good decisions.

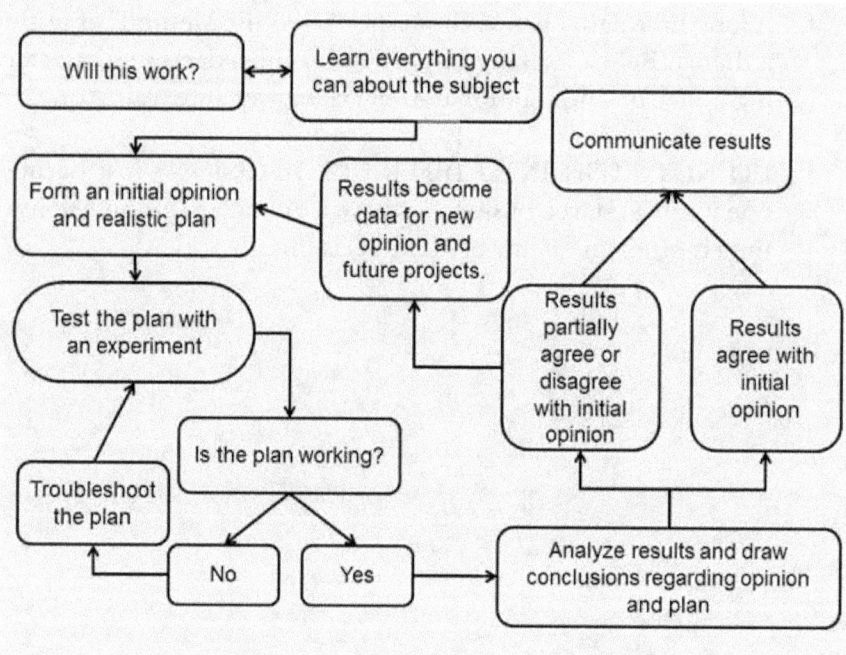

Figure 1. Applying the scientific method to a business idea and plan

LESSON 2

GET INVOLVED WITH YOUR COMPANY

*If it's your job to eat a frog, it's best to do it first
thing in the morning. And if it's your job to eat
two frogs, it's best to eat the biggest one first.*
— MARK TWAIN

What does it mean to get involved with your company?

A business owner gets up each morning and eats frogs. Those frogs may be lawsuits, customer complaints, collection problems, disgruntled employees, or other daily problems. If you have experience owning a business, you know what loneliness feels like when decisions are required. Most employees shuck hard issues, as they should, and others do not understand enough about the business to offer valid opinions.

Owners of businesses (good ones, that is), make sure all expenses, payroll and vendors are paid before they take any money from the company. Rarely in the life of a business is there sufficient money for the owner to get money every period. It takes time for the business to get established and be able to weather business problems (recessions, floods, competition, etc.). In those periods, the owner may even have to put money into the business to cover its needs. The first time the owner goes without a paycheck or has to put money into the business is when eating frogs becomes clear.

Then why do people start and buy businesses? Because if done right, the rewards are often greater than being an employee—not just monetary rewards, but the ability to make decisions, have an on-demand work schedule, or just choose co-workers.

Work everywhere

As the business owner, what do you need to do each day? What's important to a company?

Work in every department with key personnel of your company. It is easy to fall into a groove where enjoyable tasks like design or sales dominate the day. Few business owners will work to collect money from overdue invoices; that is one of the uglier, more difficult jobs. Fewer will work in the warehouse to help pick, pack, and ship orders; not all enjoy physical labor. Obviously, it is important not to devote too much time to tasks that employees can handle, but a business owner must be willing to do these tasks under certain circumstances.

Donald Thompson, former CEO at McDonald's, said on a *60 Minutes* interview that he worked at McDonald's restaurants in all capacities, including flipping burgers and cleaning bathrooms. Working every job at a company is not a necessity for running a business, but Mr. Thompson understood the inner workings in his restaurant and was able to apply that experience to the whole chain. Anyone who owns a company should not underestimate this kind of experience.

Importance of working everywhere

Companies operate more effectively when the owner knows how to do each employee's job. Employees respect owners who will work alongside them and often work harder knowing that the boss understands how to do their job. An owner will make better hiring decisions when they understand the job's tasks. Having good employees who work hard is necessary and essential for any successful business.

As a consultant, I always jumped at the chance to work in every part of a company and learn as much as I could about all aspects of business. Working in hot, non-air-conditioned factories in Mexico with a temperature of 105 degrees outside taught me how important well-placed fans could be. Unloading and packing boxes in warehouses was another task for which I earned respect from employees who, while working, often told me things about the company the owner would never have learned. If the owner learned what I knew, he or she might not have needed me.

Case Study 5 - Torreon, Mexico

One of my challenging engagements was a home-furnishing manufacturer in Torreon, Mexico. Their lender sent me to find out why the company was not making scheduled loan payments. My Spanish wasn't great, but I thought it would be an interesting job, so I took my overused passport and went to Mexico.

Torreon is in the northern part of Mexico and a short flight from Houston Texas. It is not Mexico City but a very quaint town with less traffic and a comfortable amount of energy. For my safety, it was highly recommended to use only certain taxis located at hotels or those called by trusted sources. Each meal was a culinary adventure, as menus outside of the hotel were only in Spanish; menus with pictures were much appreciated. Having the specialty of each restaurant seemed like a good bet, and this region specialized in *cabrito* (baby goat). As vegetables are mostly the same from country to country, that part was easier and cooked fresh. The "American" hotel was a 4 ½ star Crowne Plaza and very comfortable, making it easy for my first day at work.

What went wrong

Management did not pay attention to the needs in its factory, including production efficiency, quality control, and effectiveness of machinery.

Upon arriving at the manager's office, one floor above the factory, I was greeted warmly as a representative of the lender. After some routine questions about the factory, I asked the manager about his work effort on the factory floor. He was not prepared for this line of questioning, as his answers, with wandering eyes, were vague and unresponsive. I learned that he had no set schedule. (Maybe he plays in a weekly poker game that I could attend. It would be easy to see when he was bluffing!) He claimed to work often on the factory floor, but employees later reported he was rarely there, only to introduce new employees. It was disheartening to learn he generally sat in his air-conditioned office, only leaving for lunch and breaks. When he needed information for his boss, he would summon factory workers to his office. He did not know how products were made, nor could he assist if there was a manufacturing problem, and there were many.

Problems with machinery

One machine would roll out fabric until it hit a stopper. This stopper allowed the machine to measure the exact amount of fabric required to begin the process of making a comforter. Too much and the sewers would have to cut off the excess, too little and the comforter could not be made. That stopper was quite an important piece in the manufacturing process! Sometime in the past (no one remembered when), the metal piece broke and was replaced with a piece of cardboard that wore out often. I asked the manager about replacing the cardboard piece with the correct metal one. He claimed not to know there was a problem (staff behind him rolling their eyes), and asked me to show him why the part was necessary. The manager said he would look into getting a replacement part. I knew I could probably kiss my elbow before he would do that.

Problems with mechanics

Next, I met with the head mechanic and three assistants in their workshop. Repair logs that are essential to knowing when machines need repairs were void of entries for many days, as if the plant was closed. The head mechanic began his explanation with, "But Señor." (In my career working in Spanish countries, nothing good followed "But Señor".)

"But Señor, we are a bit behind in logging our work."

"How many machines do you work on each day?"

"Señor, we are busy all day." It probably will not be surprising to know the mechanics were not busy all day. They barely worked at all. Some "broken" machines just needed oil but were put in the graveyard where unusable machines go until repaired.

Some problems discovered

After working for just one week, the following was uncovered:

- Machines were not properly serviced. Many needed oil and were about to break. Some machines worked at less than full capacity; others were just broken awaiting repair. All were reparable with minor work required.
- Employees who were short in stature folded large comforters, and this resulted in dragging the comforters on the dirty factory floor. The Quality Control department (QC) rejected the damaged products and sent them to a section of the warehouse used for bad products that could not be sold. (It looked like the closing scene in Indiana Jones where the Ark of the Covenant was kept.)
- Boxes used to pack sets of sheets were too small. Each set of sheets required two people to close a packing box: one to hold the box closed and the other to tape it shut. It was funny watching one person taping another person's arm to the box because the box holder didn't move out of the way in time. One time, an employee sat on the box before realizing that his associate couldn't tape the box closed with him sitting on it.
- Factory supervisors received no instructions on what to make and decided that on their own. Often, orders were not filled completely because of this lack of control over production.

An attempt to get management to get involved

When asked if meetings with management were ever scheduled, factory workers replied, "Nunca." (Never.) After much coaxing, the factory manager finally held the company's first production meeting. The manager sat far from the exit. As the meeting became heated over his lack of concern for the employees and their work effort, I became apprehensive his position was too far from the exit for a quick escape should the employees start a riot.

Many of the workers thanked me for that meeting. They gave me a bag of M&Ms to say thanks. Perhaps my large frame made them think candy was an appropriate present, but I did appreciate the gesture. Nothing significant changed after that trip. The bank sent me back to Torreon, where I was greeted warmly by the staff and ignored by the factory manager.

The fix!

The problems uncovered were symptoms of bad management. Hearing the word "factory" often conjures up a picture of a Henry Ford type assembly line. This concept worked at the turn of the 20th century, and with enhanced modifications works today.

- In the Torreon factory, more attention needed to be paid to work schedules and output of product.
  - One solution to those problems is a scoreboard for each production line. The board has columns for expected and actual production. Results for each period (usually two hours) are reported and monitored on this board. Workers can look at the board and know how they are doing with relation to expectations. The scoreboard also acts to incentivize employees to hit daily goals in two-hour increments.
- More attention was needed in QC.
  - The solution was to implement stronger QC. If product was not completed in a saleable manner, then QC would inform production that changes would need to be made in the production line to reduce the number of damaged products.
- Mechanics didn't have service schedules that kept equipment in top form.

- The solution was to instruct mechanics to service machines more frequently, keeping them in top form. Additionally, a periodic timetable/schedule for regular maintenance schedule was created, and mechanics were instructed to record all service on the schedule.
- Meetings with key factory production personnel should have been scheduled periodically. Production staff should have been allowed to voice their opinions on improvements.
  - A meeting schedule should have been established, so that production staff could be invited and encouraged to express their opinions regarding improvements.
- Management's failure to interact with all phases of production resulted in inefficiency and poor morale.
  - The manager was encouraged to conduct walk-throughs as often as needed during the workday, to be on the lookout for problems, and to correct problems in a timely manner. Had the manager conducted such walk-ins and addressed problems, the issue with packing and shipping could have been discovered and corrected much sooner.
  - Additionally, the manager was encouraged to improve morale by showing production staff that he cared, simply by asking their opinions on improvements, not just during the meetings, but also during his walk-throughs. This is just common sense.

Key terms

Production line scoreboard: Chart listing daily goals versus actual production in a facility.

Service Schedule: A chart that lists dates for regular equipment maintenance.

Lesson 2 takeaways

- A manager should not be lazy nor fear walking through the company on a periodic basis. They may encounter a problem and not know how to immediately fix it but have the ability to eventually get the solution. Equally important are conversations with key personnel who should know they are supported to get their jobs and tasks done. The manager should always ask key personnel "How can I help you?"
- Getting out from behind the desk generally brings good results.
- Walk the factory or office floor.
- Ask all employees what they need. (At first, most will reply nothing, but the more this is done, the greater the likelihood answers will change to something useful).
- Invite employees into meetings and ask their opinions. If they have an issue, write it down (showing an interest) and then reply in a timely manner.
- Weekly meetings with staff are a great way to keep an eye on the business without being invasive with normal operations. Meetings should be beneficial for everyone, not just for the bosses to dictate and hear themselves pontificate. During mutually beneficial meetings, much is shared about the business, and the employees get empowered to do their job. Meetings can let employees know their job is important and enable management to help them do it well.
  - Be sure to avoid turning meetings into unproductive wastes of time. **Keep meetings short and on point, and leave them with actions for people to do.** Follow up meetings are sometimes helpful, as are reviews of previous meetings.
- Most important is to get involved with problems. The owner need not have all the answers all the time but needs to be there to help guide the process towards the best final decision.

Summary

The hardest job is manager; manager of anything. It not only requires one to know how to get the job done in the most efficient manner but also the psychology of dealing with people and situations. Of your managers and employees:

- Ask questions.
- Ask opinions.
- Follow up when changes are made to see they have been implemented correctly.

LESSON 3

KNOW YOUR COSTS

If there is a 50-50 chance that something will
go wrong, then 9 times out of 10 it will.
— PAUL HARVEY

An underappreciated part of businesses is the costing of products or services a company sells. The imagery one conjures about the costing department is a balding, middle-aged man wearing a green visor to shade his eyes from the exposed bright light bulb above his desk. (And, of course, the pocket protector in the shirt). Having been that person at companies, I can assure you some of my bosses would not have spent what it would cost for a bright bulb, nor a full desk.

Agreed, costing is boring but so valuable to a company that many of my consulting assignments originated because clients could not figure their costs, thus causing losses. They knew how much money sales brought the company, which they could track by looking at the cash in the bank account. Expenses were easy to determine by total checks paid for ongoing bills. Checks paid to vendors baffled them, however. The clients could add up these amounts to determine how much in total they had paid to vendors, but understanding how these payments related to profits *per product or service* alluded them. Most attempts at calculating the cost of a product were generally wrong, and they abandoned their efforts for lack of accuracy. Without knowing the costs, management searched for reasons causing losses but could not make a correct determination.

What is costing?

Costing is the accumulation of money spent to complete a product to sell to customers. Costing gets a bit confusing because a true analysis includes all costs related to produce the product, ship to a destination and all expenses in between. Often those preparing the reports forget items like travel to a factory to help production or the salaries of design staff, or warehouse personnel who received and store product and other less prominent expenses. Companies often forget incidentals that may be small in nature and cost but, nevertheless, are part of the total cost.

An easy way to understand what should be included in the cost of a product is as follows:

Cost = *__Every expense associated with getting the product to a saleable state.__*

Why is costing important?

Accurately knowing what products and services cost allows management to charge a competitive and profitable price. When deciding on a price for a product, one of the major factors is the cost to make that product. Management needs to cover:

1. The cost to make the product
2. Overhead items like rent, utilities, telephone, etc.

Amounts in excess of 1 and 2 above are the company's profit.

What if the company miscalculates the cost of the product?

Below is a quick example of how product costing can get off track.

	Incorrect Costing	Correct Costing
Sale price	1,000	1,000
Product cost	(800)	(850)
Overhead	(175)	(175)
Total costs	(975)	(1,025)
Profit (loss)	25	(25)

Table 3. Impact of incorrect product costing

The correct scenario shows a $25 loss on a product. This would exist if the product costs are miscalculated. Without realizing the sales price needs adjustment to cover _all_ costs, the company assumes it is making a $25 profit on the product. Note that overhead apportioned to the product is the same. It is quite easy to know overhead in most cases. For example, the rent does not change, and telephone is a somewhat constant expense, as are insurance, payroll, and many other recurring expenses.

Sometimes a product is priced similar to competitor's products. In this case, knowing the cost of the product is essential to achieving profits because the competitor's price restricts the sales price. When a competitor's product is not an important focus, the product cost helps management to determine what the selling price should be.

If costs are not accurate, products offered for sale may be too expensive or too cheap. Either way, inaccurate costing puts the company at a distinct disadvantage that usually causes losses.

What products or services cost may seem easy to determine, but none of my clients have been able to accomplish this task. How difficult could it be? Very difficult! Many clients wanted to know why they were losing money, and that is what prompted them to engage my services. An example of a common error is failing to include the cost of boxes and tape necessary for shipping a product to a customer. Some call it a shipping expense, but I would refer you back to the definition of a cost: _Every_ *expense associated with getting the product to a saleable state.* Since my client's product could not be shipped without the box and tape, those supplies are essential and necessary for the sale and should be included in the total cost of getting the product to the customer.

Costing is like chess, in that it's easy to learn and difficult to master. Understanding costing will give you a better chance at success in business because you must know the true cost of a product in order to determine the gross profit (as shown in the Table 1 example).

Profits are calculated as follows:

Gross Profit = Revenue - Cost of Goods

Gross profit (or revenue) is the amount of money a company earns from the sale of its products or services after paying product costs (cost of goods). The company uses gross profits to pay for overhead items like rent, salaries, and insurance. Any money remaining after paying overhead is net profit to the company. If the gross profit of a company is not sufficient to pay all overhead costs, losses occur, and changes are necessary.

Note: Expenses like rent fall into the category of overhead because they are not essential to making the product. One can make a product without having an office or insurance.

Raise the bridge or lower the water

Consider the profits of a company as a boat trying to sail under a bridge. If the company has losses, it needs to either raise the bridge (increase gross profit) or lower the water (reduce overhead) or a combination of both. Even if a company has profits and the boat can sail under the bridge, it still can raise the bridge more or lower the water more to increase its profits.

To make a business more successful, a company can:

- Increase revenue (get more sales)
- Decrease overhead (lower rent, telephone, etc.)
- Decrease cost of goods (lower the cost to make the product)

Revenue is hard to change. Every company is trying to increase revenue but can only charge what customers are willing to pay. Getting new customers and orders is what every company tries to do. Competition makes increasing revenue more difficult as do the limited resources of a company. There is just so much money a company can spend on advertising to attract new customers. Overhead is fairly easy to reduce, but a company should already be running with as little overhead as possible. That leaves cost of goods sold (COGS) as the most promising area to focus on to increase profits.

Focus on COGS to save money

Cost of goods sold (look back at the definition for cost if you don't remember it) is the best and often the easiest place to become more efficient. Because cost of goods sold is usually where a company spends most of its money, it seems only logical to try and reduce disbursements. A company can spend 70 percent of its total revenue creating and producing products. Negotiating and expanding the number of vendors, thereby creating a competition for your business, can result in significant cost savings. By letting vendors know you are interested in obtaining a lower price, you are giving them an opportunity to understand they should offer the best price to get your business.

What if a company incorrectly calculates its gross profit?

Case Study 6 – Paperco(Pco)

A client purchased seconds of paper products from paper mills. They resold the seconds to printers who did not need perfect, first quality paper for their printing jobs. For example, printers might be printing place mats in diners, which did not require quality paper.

Each month, the client would diligently review his sales and profit numbers expecting his accountant to confirm his findings. Every month, the accountant brought bad news; the figures were worse than the business records. After many months of this exercise, the accountant called to ask if I could review the company's records to locate the difference in the numbers. He believed the error was in the Gross Profit calculation, and more specifically, in the cost of the paper—that is, every expense associated with getting the product to the printers (a saleable state).

And, indeed, after a short time of reviewing the records, it became evident that the client's calculation of cost did not include every expense associated with getting the product to the printers (a saleable state).

What went wrong

Examination of records showed several areas in which product costs were inaccurately estimated:

- Commission costs were higher than anticipated
  - The company paid more to its salespersons in total, which included commission, travel expenses, health benefits, and more.
- Freight costs to bring paper to the warehouse were estimated; actual costs were greater
  - Because freight invoices from truckers were received generally 10-15 days after delivery, the company estimated the costs so that they could immediately calculate the cost and know how much to sell the goods for. Received invoices, as it turned out, often included multiple deliveries of paper. Pco had not analyzed the invoices and broken down each delivery to determine if their estimates for costs of specific products they'd already sold were correct. Underestimations of the freight cost caused the company to charge customers less than it should have. Had Pco known the cost of freight was higher than their estimates, their prices to the printers would have increased accordingly.
- Warehousing and storage costs also were underestimated
  - An independent warehouse was responsible for receiving, picking, packing and shipping paper for the client. They charged fees for all services, including storage in a warehouse. Pco did not correctly analyze the month's end invoice

from the warehouse. Each month, the warehouse counted unsold paper still stored and charged Pco a storage fee. Despite the low cost to house the paper, it nevertheless resulted in some fee that would not have been charged if Pco had sold the paper. That fee should have been added to the cost of the paper but was not. Because the company did not calculate this expense in the product's cost, Pco suffered a degradation in profits when the stored paper sold.

Example of where Pco got off-track with their costing:

A unit of paper costing 17 cents per pound was not sold for 6 months. Storage costs, if applied to that unit, would have brought the total cost to 18 cents per pound, just one cent more. That doesn't seem like much, does it? In reality, it makes a significant difference in profits.

	Incorrect Costing	Correct Costing
Sale price per pound	$0.22	$0.22
Product cost	$0.17	$0.18
Gross Profit (loss)	$0.05	$0.04
Percent profit on sale price	22.7%	18.2%

Table 4. Comparison of profitability

Just one penny difference caused a 4.5% drop in the percentage of gross profit!

Why is that important?

If the company had 1 million dollars in sales and lost 4.5% on each sale because of poor costing and selling practices, the difference would result in a $ 45,000 loss for every million dollars made in sales.

The company's policy was to achieve a 22% margin on all sales, which accounted for overhead of 18%, leaving 4% for profit. For every sale in which the cost of the product was actually higher than estimated and the resulting Gross Profit was 4.5% lower than estimated, the company lost money. Had Pco known the actual cost of the paper, including storage costs, was 18 cents, it could have charged 23 cents for the paper, thereby earning 5 cents or 21.7% profit on the sale. That profit would cover the 18% overhead and leave 3.7% gross profit. On sales of 1 million dollars, their profitability would change from negative $45,000 to a positive $37,000.

The fix

First and foremost, the company needed to work harder at calculating freight costs and applying that result to more accurately invoice customers. This step is first because each day freight costs are not correctly charged to customers causes immediate losses.

Recalculating the cost of unsold paper in the warehouse, although important, would not cause a loss until a sale. The company, therefore, had some time to adjust the costing and sales price of the items in inventory.

The results of this one fix changed the costs of all paper in the computer system, allowing the client to set prices more effectively to achieve the 22% needed for reasonable profitability.

Case Study 7 – Moon City Apparel

Moon City Apparel was an apparel "manufacturer" with approximately 60 million US dollars in sales. I used quotes around the word manufacturer because they "caused" manufacturing to be done and did not have company-owned and -worked factories. Factories in China produced all of the goods for Moon City Apparel.

Moon City Apparel was in a very competitive market. Their niche was selling garments to big box stores which, in turn, would sell the apparel for $19.95. The cost to product a garment ranged from $6 to $9, and the price charged to the big box store varied. The goal was to achieve about a 22% gross profit. Overhead was 18%, and the 4% remaining would result in a $2.4 million profit at the end of the year.

How important was knowing the costs of the product for Moon City Apparel? Crucial!

Because apparel was manufactured in China, a host of costs needed to be added to the total cost of a garment. Some items differ from costing in a company-owned and -operated factory.

These additional costs include:

- Payroll for the design team
- Rent for the design team
- Fabric, buttons, and trim used in all samples sent to the factory overseas
- Shipping to send specifications to the factory
- Travel for a company representative to the factory to review production
- Shipping to import the finished goods
- Duty and broker fees for the goods to clear customs
- Shipping to bring the goods from the pier to the warehouse
- Payroll for the warehouse team to receive the finished goods
- Rent for the portion of the warehouse used to store the finished goods
- Commission for the salesperson

Additional notes:

- The company representative's trip to the factory and the salesperson's commission may not have been added to the making of the final product, but should be included because they were part of the sale. Commission for the salesperson is included as an example because companies often assign customers to a specific salesperson and, thereby, pay commission to the assigned salesperson on all related sales.

- Licensing – If a company licenses a product image or name (i.e., Disney characters or a designer apparel name), it pays a percentage of sales to the licensor. That fee must be paid for each sale and, therefore, should be included in the total cost of a product.

There may be more unusual costs like those above, and if so, they should be included, as well. It is important for management to identify those costs and include them into the total cost of a product (COGS).

What went wrong

Moon City Apparel did not account for all costs associated with the manufacturing of garments and, consequently, experienced losses that caused the company to cease operations.

In addition to the incorrectly calculated COGS, Moon City Apparel also suffered losses suffered because garments were:

1. Sold for a price less than cost
2. Unsaleable for a variety of reasons. These unsaleable items were warehoused at great expense. There was little chance of selling these goods, and abandonment was a better option.
3. Received in an unsaleable manner from the manufacturer in China, who was reluctant to negotiate appropriate credits. Because Moon City Apparel *needed* the manufacturer to continue supplying goods, they had a reduced ability to negotiate for credits.

What is the impact of the above on a costing system?

All of the above losses need to be added to the costing of each garment. If the losses equate to 1/2 of a percent of the company's total sales, then each garment must carry its share of that loss. A garment that would cost $7.00 without the 1/2% "cushion" must now cost $7.05 with the loss included. Knowing this, the company could look for cost savings in other areas to offset this loss or adjust its expectations on profitability, but NOT be surprised by outcomes.

Key terms

Cost of goods sold (COGS): All costs associated with getting a product sold.

Gross profit: Revenue minus cost of goods sold.

Overhead: All expenses not related to creating or getting a product to the customer.

Revenue: Income from product sale.

Lesson 3 takeaways

- Correct costing requires that all expenses necessary to get the product to market are included in the COGS. It sounds simple, but it's very easy to forget or overlook some expenses.
- Update costings periodically, at least every six months or more often if costs are rising.
- Take a sample of invoices and review costing and profit on each. The goal is to either:
  - Validate the costing system is correct or
  - Learn why the system is incorrect and make the necessary changes for the future.
- Management can make positive changes by reviewing costs.
- As opposed to rent or telephone expenses that are hard to change, finding alternative suppliers of raw materials can make a large positive difference in a company's profitability. Even if satisfied with a vendor, periodically look for others whose prices and quality may be the same.

Summary

Despite the often confusing nature of numbers in accounting, one must recognize the importance of knowing company costs. The word essential does not do justice to the crucial nature of this knowledge. A company can only have in overhead an amount equal to or less than the gross profits earned from the sale of products or services.

If a company makes $100 gross profit from selling a product, only that amount can be spent for rent, utilities, telephone, salaries, etc. If more is spent, the company will need additional cash to cover the short-fall of profits. That additional cash usually comes from a bank. We'll take a look at banking later in this book.

LESSON 4

MONEY AND POSSESSION

I don't like lending money to people because
then they have it and I don't.
— DAVE FERRAR

D ave Ferrar is not a finance guru. He's actually a horse trainer
and didn't know how prophetic his statement was. It's a simple
statement but useful across many situations. Throughout this
chapter, remember the wisdom of Dave Ferrar.

Why is the possession of money so important?

Without money, a business will most likely fail. (Sorry, but the obvious
has to be stated to begin the understanding of how important possessing
money is to the livelihood of a business.) If this statement is true (and it
is), then what causes businesses to not have money? If we could solve this
problem, the bankruptcy and insolvency rate among businesses would
drop precipitously.

Here are a few items that cause businesses not to have money:

- Accounts receivable, credit, and collection
- Inventory (covered in chapter 7)
- Business losses
- Capital expenditures (purchasing of equipment and large items)
- Other

Accounts receivable, credit, and collection

What are accounts receivable?

Accounts receivable are sales made by a company for which the customer did not pay at the time of sale but will (hopefully) pay at a later date. It is very important to recognize the company can say no to issuing credit. If management believes there is too much risk in issuing credit, it should not do so. It is better to have the product than sell it on credit and not get paid; otherwise, the customer has both the product and your money. The only way to know if the company made a good decision on issuing credit is the "post-mortem": the customer paid.

What does it mean to issue credit to a customer?

Credit represents the company's belief their customer will pay for product or services at a future date. Companies usually have their customer complete a credit application to include details about the customer, i.e. how long in business, references who could vouch for the customer's credibility, etc. There is a dichotomy about issuing credit. Sales executives are assigned tasks to sell and increase business while the accounting department's responsibility is to collect the money. Usually the sales staff are upset when they get a sale only to have it nixed by the credit department. When the credit department takes a risk that does not work out, it makes both the credit department and management suffer. Management is, again, in control of this process and can blame no one if/when customers do not pay. It can say no.

The cleanup: collection

Collection takes place after credit has been issued and a sale made. It is the cleanup part of the process when the company waits until the invoice becomes due then collects the money. During this process, the company is not in control, having passed their goods/services to the customer who now has both the product and money. The company is in control of the process by which it collects the money and keeps good relations with customers to get future orders.

Remember Dave Ferrar, who believes in having control over the money. With the customer having control over both the money and product/service, the company's role changes from master to servant. It needs to cautiously work with the customer to insure the best chance of collection. Company collection efforts need to be professional, tranquil, and focused, fully understanding how tenable a situation issuing credit actually is.

What if a company does not have money?

What if the company's policy for issuing credit and the subsequent collection process is flawed and causes the company to lose money? What could cause a company to not have money? Many events and issues could cause a company to have insufficient money to operate a business. Among them are:

- Losses caused by company inefficiencies
- Poor collections processes of accounts receivable
- Too much unsold inventory
- Capital expenditures (purchase of machinery or equipment)
- Law suits that cause excess professional fees and maybe a judgement
- And many more

What would happen to a company that does not have sufficient cash?

All of the problems one could imagine would exist if a company does not have money, including:

- Employees leaving because they have not been paid
- Vendors not shipping new merchandise because of non-payment
- And everything in between

The essential part to understand, and I cannot overstate its importance, is *the timing of obtaining money when needed.* When money is needed, it is usually urgent and required now.

A bank loan takes some time to get and could delay a business event that is crucial to the existence of the business. Owners often have money that is not liquid and need time to cash in non-liquid assets or obtain cash. It is important to know where money would come from if needed.

Without money, a company must acquire it. Among the most popular ways to get money into a company are:

- The owners could put money into the business.
- A bank loan could be arranged.
- The company could sell part of its ownership interest (shares).

None of the above are as good as management working hard to insure it has available cash.

Money from Owners

Although this is the least expensive of the options, it should be carefully weighed to insure the money could be repaid. This is like the cavalry that is kept in reserve until needed to fight. The reserve, once used, cannot be called upon again, so make sure it is called in an appropriate, timely manner. An example of when to use a reserve might be when replacing product damaged by a flood while waiting for an insurance claim to be filed and money received.

A bank loan

Bank loans are quite dangerous if management does not understand all of the trappings. If one were to look across the USA in just about any town, they would find banks make up a large part of the landscape. Who is paying the salaries of the employees of the bank, its rent, lights, etc.? How about the administration of the bank, its managers, executives, officers and many more people who are paid? People who borrow money are the key candidates who support the profits of the bank.

Sell part of the company / take an investor
Without delving into an often worse option than taking a bank loan, it is very important to understand the many negatives of taking on an investor or selling part of the business.

Here are just some of the major negatives:

1. Once an investor knows the company "needs" help, they usually get a disproportionately greater share of the ownership.
2. An investor, by law, has rights in court as a minority shareholder that could interfere with the operations of the business.
3. If a majority of the company is sold, by that definition, control over the company is lost. This occurs even when the minority shareholder's ideas are better.

Case Study 8 – Steel convertor
One who needs a loan is at the mercy of the lender. For the money received (loan) the lender wants something in return. The person with the money can do what they want with it, and therein lies the rub. The needier (or more desperate) the borrower, the more onerous the terms of the loan.

A client's business was two generations old, and despite losing money, it was surviving. The owners were serious about staying in business, reducing their salaries and all expenses necessary to make payroll and pay vendors on time. Their lender, Wells Fargo, was going through a restructuring event. Wells told my client to find another lender; they would not be renewing the line of credit.

What went wrong
Nothing, but Wells' need to restructure caused this change. The client did nothing wrong but was in the wrong place (wrong bank) and at the

wrong time. Wells classified the loan as "performing," meaning, among other things, all principal and interest payments were made on time. The timing could not have been worse for the client. Getting a new lender would be very difficult because of losses suffered in recent times. It was like sending a Florida resident to the outer reaches of Russian Siberia… in winter.

New lenders believed the loan to be questionable. Wells had a good history with the company over many years, but new lenders did not and were worried about the ability of the company to pay the loan and interest. The company was now needier than it had been when with Wells, and new lenders willing to take a chance on the company wanted large closing fees (like when closing on a house). Tens of thousands of dollars in fees were requested to make the loan. In addition to the exorbitant fees, other covenants or conditions were included in the loan agreement, making it more difficult for the company to operate successfully. With few choices, the company paid the fees, agreed to the covenants, and took the loans.

What was the effect?

- Executive's normal business activity was diminished in the process of finding, negotiating, and closing a new loan.
- Fees paid to the new lender were excessive and reduced cash available for business operations, like paying vendors and taking advantage of cash deals for product.
- New bank covenants (promises made by the business about its performance) were put in place, causing changes in the business operationally and financially. If the business did not meet those promises, the lender could charge additional fees and ask the client to leave.
  - With each covenant broken by the customer, the lender was able to charge additional fees. The more covenants put in place at the time of the loan, the greater potential for the lender to make more money. An example of a bank covenant might be having current assets greater than current liabilities

but a ratio of 1.5 to 1. In the life of a business, this may not always be true but could be for 4 out of 5 particular years. If in the 5th year, the ratio falters, the lender may charge an additional fee.

Side note about lenders and their fees

It seems to be in the lender's best interest to make as many new loans as possible. With each new loan, they get a new closing fee, and that is in addition to the interest earned on the loan. From a business perspective, a lender should try to make as many new loans as possible to earn the closing fees. It might also be in their interest to terminate and collect existing loans, using those proceeds to make new loans and receive new closing fees, in essence, an incentive not to renew existing loans.

The fix

In the Steel convertor's case, little could be done to overcome a negative outside influence (Wells).

In most cases, a business needs to adjust its cash requirements to avoid situations like the above. When cash is tight:

- Slow down on issuing credit to new customers, continuing with existing good customers.
- Buy less inventory even if it means not taking advantage of discounts offered for purchasing greater quantities.

Back to Dave Ferrar's theory

The lesson to be learned from the above example is the "possession" of money. Having it allows greater flexibility to make good decisions for a company, and not having it requires servitude in various forms. This is not to say that bank loans are all bad and never should be taken but to emphasize the importance of managing cash as one would a precious asset.

Case study 9: Costume jewelry wholesaler

Business Losses

A lender called one day to ask if I could visit with one of their clients who needed some consulting help. The business was selling costume jewelry manufactured in Asia to retailers in the USA. Kohl's was their largest customer. Revenue and profits were good for many years until they hit a bump in the road. Actually, the speed bump was quite large and almost caused the business to fail.

What went wrong

In 2006, in Minneapolis, a young boy of 4 years old swallowed a piece of costumer jewelry and died of lead poisoning. (http://www.medpagetoday.com/Pediatrics/GeneralPediatrics/2966).

Laws were changed to stop the use of lead in costume jewelry. The company had to discontinue selling jewelry manufactured with lead. It also advised its customers to return all product that contained lead. Kohl's alone returned over $ 400,000 of product. The manufacturer in Asia would not take the jewelry back because it had filled orders per the request of the company.

The company was forced to both throw away the jewelry with lead and purchase all new costume jewelry without lead. A large amount of money was needed to make the new purchases.

The fix

Normally this type of event is so catastrophic as to cause most companies to fail. In this case, the company survived because it had profits and cash available to survive until new costume jewelry arrived without lead to replace the returned merchandise.

Our job was to provide the lender with financial projections showing the impact of the loss. Using the company's cash in the bank and its projected cash from accounts receivable, a report was created to determine how much additional cash would be required for the company to stay in business. Final projections were submitted to the lender with a request for a short-term loan. Because the payback was relatively fast, the lender agreed. Business went on as normal, profits were made, the bank paid back on schedule, and the company was able to continue in business.

A true success story was accomplished because the business had cash and profits, allowing the lender to help keep the business alive and not have to force its closure.

Key terms

Accounts receivable: Sales made by a company for which the customer did not pay at the time of sale but promises to pay for at a later date.

Bank Covenants: Performance restrictions on the lender, contractually agreed to by the borrower, that are reviewed periodically. If not met penalties (usually financial) are charged.

Projections: Financial reports that estimate future operations of a business, i.e. cash collections, sales, expenses. The purposes include:

- The creation of a plan that management can accept as practical and sound
- Subsequent review of the plan validating its practicality
- An offering to potential lenders inducing them to make a loan
- And much more.

Lesson 4 takeaways

It is essential to have some cash reserves in case a situation like the above occurs. The reserve need not be in the form of actual cash in the bank but the availability of cash. This could be in the form of cash, stocks, CD's or other financial instruments in the owner's personal bank account that are available if needed. A line of credit could be made available as well, separate from the business, for such need.

Summary

- All too often, all money is used or taken from corporate bank accounts, thereby limiting options.
- All efforts should be made to allow outside interests (i.e. banks and vendors) to have a comfort level the business can pay its debts.

LESSON 5

CREDIT

The problem with issuing credit

Issuing credit might be compared with owning a rare, old, valuable book that someone wants to borrow. Although the issuance of credit is not a tangible item like a book, it has the same negative fear: what if the book is not returned, what if the credit is not paid back? In both cases, a loss has occurred. If too many of the credit type losses occur, the business will suffer greatly.

The handshake – or not

Customers want product and are willing to pay money for it. If they pay the full amount up front, the company has experienced an "equal" transaction; it sold goods and received money. If the company issues credit, the customer has both the product and the money, which is an unequal transaction. The company has to wait to get paid. Dave Ferrar would say, "Now they have my money, and I don't." The customer's ability to pay is predicated on their business acumen and ability to operate a successful business. As the issuer of credit, the company has little control over this and is at risk every time credit is issued. It is very important to recognize that issuing credit can be a normal business practice that is good for all, but also that bad business partners will make one cringe at issuing more credit. Try to figure out what kind of partner you're working with up front.

Case Study 10 – California Roofing and Gutter Company

In 2010, I was in sunny California working with a roofing and gutter company that had 10 branch locations and extended $35 million in credit each year. The home office did not have a policy for determining credit worthiness. Rather, they left that decision solely to branch managers. If a customer didn't pay on time, the home office's advice was to talk to a local collection attorney for help. Setting up a credit policy was one of the first projects to change.

What went wrong

Branch managers had a dual role of obtaining new orders and collecting on old ones. Can you guess which was more important when speaking with management? If you guessed new sales, you were correct. The focus for branch managers was on new sales only.

Outstanding accounts receivable erupted into large amounts ($900,000), some of it old and hard to collect. Branch managers did not know what to do except to hire collection agencies and lawyers and hope for the best.

The company did not have sufficient capital to pay vendors and had difficulty meeting payroll. It had to look to other sources for money. Because of a lack of capital, the owners had to sell the company for very little. Were the outstanding accounts receivable the total cause of the company's need to sell? Not entirely, but they certainly contributed to the need to sell.

The fix

The new owners engaged my services and implemented a new plan for managing credit and collections. When the project was complete, less than 1% of credit was uncollectible in an industry in which the normal loss was about 5%. Management considered this a big success. The plan was anchored on changing policies, beginning with the reduction of managers' involvement, allowing fewer distractions, which, in turn, allowed them to focus solely on selling new roofs and gutters.

What changes were made to effect the success? A two-part approach was conceived and implemented.

Part 1 - Add an additional guarantor

The new plan added two clauses to the existing credit agreement. The first clause added a personal guarantee to help insure collection if the customer did not pay. Often the credit application was completed by a corporation. If the corporation went out of business, it would be difficult to collect. With the customer personally guaranteeing payment, there was a greater chance of collection. Corporations go out of business, but people generally do not. Also, with this personal guarantee in place, a customer might pay the company before others who do not have this in place. The second clause gives the company a lien on any unsold inventory and allows for recovery if the product sold still exists in the customer's inventory, thereby cutting losses.

Part 2 – Become more efficient at issuing credit to good companies

This part is customary and usual but not so at the Roofing and Gutter company. Standard information provided by the customer in the credit application it submitted was sent to a credit service like Experian, Transunion, or Equifax. These agencies provide essential information on the customer's history—from how many years in business to a listing of on-time and late payments. Most companies use this information to make credit decisions—i.e., reported late payments might be a sign not to issue any credit. Credit services charge a small fee for this service, but that minor charge could potentially save significantly more than money if just one modest loss is avoided.

What to look for on the credit application

One very important factor in issuing credit is the *amount of time a customer has been in business.* My policy is to award many bonus points for those companies that have been in business over 10 years. If they can make it that long, they deserve not only some credit but maybe some medals, as well.

A business's credit worthiness is similar to a person's. A perfect credit history isn't required to be credit worthy. Sometimes a bill or payment gets lost in the mail. I believe any person who has a steady income and is living within their means is probably worthy of credit. The same is true for a corporation. As long as they *have been in business for many years and pay their bills somewhat on time,* they are deserving of some credit.

There are additional factors when considering issuing credit for a business. Unlike an employee who gets one check each week to deposit, most businesses get many and hope all will clear their bank. Again, as stated many times above, a business' success is predicated upon the ability of its customers to also operate successfully.

If an employee gets a paycheck, deposits it in the bank, and pays bills using that money, only to find that payroll check bounced, all of the bills paid by that person also bounce. It appears to be a multi-calamitous event with many vendors charging fees and calling for money, yet a singular event caused the multiple problems: one payroll check bouncing.

The same could happen to a business with either a large customer check bouncing or a transfer not being made into a bank account. When issuing credit, one should *try to understand bad marks on a credit report before declining credit.* A credit application can always be declined, but it might help to call the applicant and ask questions. If the answers are still not satisfactory, then one may decline knowing all was done to help the company get an order from a good risk.

The PW effect

As the CFO at companies, my job often included the credit and collection part of the business. In one company, orders were taken by my boss, PW. My job was to submit orders to a factoring company that would approve or decline the order. The factoring company guaranteed the financial ability of the customer to pay, so if they did not, the factor paid on behalf of the customer. PW was not a risk taker, so all orders were submitted to the factor for approval. My job was easy, in that most orders received a credit approval. When an order was declined, my job was to argue with the credit analyst or his manager to get a credit approval. If not, the order would not be completed and the company would certainly lose the order and maybe all the customer's business.

On my lazy days, I would bring the declined order to PW and explain that the factor declined the order. PW would look at me and say, "Neil, anyone can call in an order and have it declined. I can have the local bum down the street tell me that. I need you to get the approval." He was right. Anyone, literally anyone, could bring him a decline. He needed someone to fight to get the approval, the order, and the profits for the company. With my tail between my legs, I returned to my office and fought to get credit approvals from the factor.

Future conversations with PW on declines came with much information about how hard I tried to get an approval and why the customer did not deserve it. PW had the ability and authority to ship the goods but with no safety net if the customer did not pay. At that point, more discussions with the customer ensued, and often we often shipped the goods with the mere hope of subsequent payment.

Lesson learned from the PW effect

Most companies have a difficult time just getting an order. The credit and collection departments need to work equally hard to insure the order meets company standards for credit. It might mean making a visit to the customer's premises or telephone calls to clarify a particular issue on the credit application. Regardless, all efforts need to be made to get the approval and subsequent cash collection.

Negative effects of issuing bad credit

The domino effect of not collecting

When a company makes a mistake when issuing credit, few good things occur thereafter. Goods are shipped with specific terms for the customer to pay. The company expects to receive payment on time or in a relatively short period thereafter (a few days). Not being paid on time can have many negative effects on a company. Company bills may not be paid on time, and relationships with vendors may deteriorate. Any time spent collecting money is time not spent on other things, like creating new business. An extra employee may be required to contact customers about timely payments. Constantly hearing about collection problems may make the company too cautious about giving credit, even to companies that would pay on time.

Why this is important
As outlined in great detail in this chapter, money is one of the keys to keeping a business secure and solvent. Issuing credit to unworthy customers is the slippery slope of decline. Company product is in the hands of customers who also have the money. It takes valuable company resources (personnel and time) to collect and reduces focus on operating successfully.

Points to review when issuing credit

In business how long?
One of the biggest factors in issuing credit is the amount of time that a company has been in business. It's said that in any 10-year period, a company will have 3 good years, 3 bad years, and 4 mediocre years. Good business owners put money away during the good years to make it through the bad years. It's not uncommon for a company to have trouble paying bills at some point. There are many things that can go wrong at a company: customers not paying bills, product problems, employee problems, etc. Good companies eventually pay, even if late, and stay in business. A company that's been around more than 10 years has made it through a few bad years, and that alone may make it worthy of consideration for credit.

The drunk and the lamppost
Credit reports should be reviewed with caution. As the adage goes, a drunk uses a lamppost for support, not light.

The exact opposite is true for companies issuing credit using Reporting Service Companies. They should use the report for light, but not support. In essence, *do not use the report as the only source when making a decision but as part of the guidance* (the light, not support).

Some companies do business overseas, and reporting services generally do not have this information available. These companies could be great risks, but their credit reports could be quite limited and not reflect that fact.

People's personal lives may affect their businesses
All economies have ups and downs because of recessions and boom markets. Between 2003 and 2008, the economy grew rapidly and housing markets blossomed. One need not have been a genius in real estate to make money during that time. One could pick just about any house to buy, and within a short period of time, it was worth more than the purchase price. Other factors governed over this rapid increase, mainly the lenders' ability to provide mortgages.

In July of 1996, the Dow Jones average was in the low 8,000's. By September of 2007, it had reached just under 16,000. By February 2009, it was again around 8,000.

How many people (who also own business) were heavily invested in both the stock market and real estate? The answer is many, and losses were suffered that affected not only personal, but also business lives.

Bonus Credit points
*** When reviewing a business that began before 2009, I give an extra point of credit worthiness to those who survived that period. I made telephone calls to some customers seeking credit whose credit reports showed late payments and disputes. The major question asked was how they made it through 2009-2010. Answers ranged from hard to very

difficult, but they persevered, and that counts for much. They did not give up; their business success was important to them, and, consequently, paying bills was one of the events to make that so.

Case Study 11 - Furniture Store

Credit looks good

Nostradamus would be great at telling whether a company is worthy of credit. Combine that with Sherlock Holmes' penchant for details, and you have the perfect couple for assessing credit worthiness. For example, a furniture company wants to place an order for $25,000 worth of your product (lighting fixtures) and is asking to pay in 30 days. Their credit application says they have $3 million in revenue and have been in business for 6 years. A credit report from one of the agencies shows they usually pay vendors on time. Everything looks good at the outset.

The Wrench

Let's throw a wrench into this scenario. Although the credit report shows timely payments, none of the invoices were for an amount greater than $10,000. This detail may be hard to see if you aren't looking for it, but it's important. If they have $3 million in revenue, they are probably purchasing at least $1.5 million in product. That's $120k each month. One might expect to see at least one vendor issuing credit above $10,000. Where are they buying their fixtures? Are they paying cash? Are vendors not reporting to agencies?

What could go wrong and how to avoid it

By not investigating fully, key elements of the credit analysis might be missed. Although the $25,000 order might seem like a good one to take from a sales and profit perspective, the possibility of not collecting should make management cautious.

Ways to get additional information and make a good credit decision include:

- Call the customer and ask about their relationship with vendors who gave $10,000 of credit or more.
- Ask how much the customer usually purchases from vendors, the terms, and whether they can be called for a reference. It's possible the biggest vendors were not listed on the credit application because their relationship is a trade secret. (One client manufactured intimate apparel with a special padding that was sold by only two companies in the USA. It would not have been prudent to list that vendor on a credit report for fear others might find the "secret".)
- Call the references and ask for any information available on the customer, from the number of years of experience to high credit issued and question about their overall relationship.
- It's unlikely that any intelligent person would put a bad reference on the list, but it's still a good idea to call. If one reference were to be a plant, such a friend or relative posing as a reference, that's a big warning sign not to extend credit.
  - One trick to use is to ask vendors how long they have been servicing the customer. If they say 10 years and the customer's credit application only shows 5 years in business, be very aware of a planted reference.
- Good questions involve asking about credit history and responsiveness. A late payment or two is not a big problem if the customer has a history of prompt payment. Ask if the customer answers the telephone all the time or hides when invoices are past due.
- Pay attention to any answer before which the responder hesitates or answers in an evasive manner. People are often reluctant to give bad references, but, nevertheless, will usually tell the truth when asked. If you call a reference and ask whether the company always pays on time, an answer like "yes, usually" or "yes, they've turned things around recently" warrants further investigation.

Some other reasons to decline credit if unsure about the customer:

- The goods can be sold to a better credit risk.
- If by shipping a new order, the total owed would exceed your comfort level.
  - This occurs when you have set a credit limit for a customer who wishes additional purchases above that amount. Sometimes the previous invoices are not due, and it becomes difficult to ask a customer for an early payment. It may come across as a lack of trust.
- The shipment to the customer will be in such quantity they need not order for many months. This might put the company in a precarious position of having its customer in an excessively powerful position. The customer would have both the product and the money.

Case Study 12 – Pco Paper

Pco Paper sold all types of paper to printing companies who used the paper for magazines, flyers, and a variety of other jobs.

What went wrong – Credit issued to weak businesses.

A group of Pco's customers had outstanding invoices that were not paid until the company sent a new shipment. It was not hard to determine the customers were not able to pay for the first order because they needed proceeds from the new shipment to pay the old invoice. It appeared the customer was using the money earned from the new order to pay for the previous order, which was a vicious cycle that would not change unless the customer improved their business.

Two choices

Unfortunately, Pco had two choices: stop shipping orders and lose the money that was owed or continue shipping orders and hope to get paid.

Eventually, if the customer did not improve their business, all would be lost. Pco did not agree with this philosophy. To prove my point, I offered to visit seven of the worst offenders with the Pco CFO. My client was enthusiastic about this process, as he would learn about his customers and my commitment to his business.

After visiting all seven customers, the CFO was convinced all were bad risks and warned his boss about offering too much credit in the future to this group. My client then asked what could be done to unwind a bad credit situation.

Not shipping more product would certainly lead to an awkward, if not legal and costly, collection process of outstanding amounts due. Continuing to ship would not solve the long-term problem.

The fix

The needed solution was simple: Continue to sell to this group but begin to whittle down the older balance with each order. A plan was developed to ship new product to the existing customers (thereby keeping an ongoing relationship with them), collect older invoices, and achieve a comfort level that new shipments would be paid for in a timely manner.

The customer paid for the "new" invoice in full plus 2% to 5% of the old invoice. For practical purposes, the plan treated the old invoice as a loan to be paid off over time. (See schedule in Table 5 below.) If a new order was $ 500.00, the customer might only have to include $ 25.00 extra against the old invoice. It may seem like a small amount, but multiply that over many orders and the old balance due might be paid in full. Without this time-extended arrangement, the old balance would have likely remained at 100% of the total owed.

My client was able to collect a little extra money, which is always good. The customers were not hit with a large penalty and were able to stay in business. In a few months, they caught up and were in good standing. In the short term, the new payment plan netted an additional $162.50 collected in just a couple of months.

Date	New Invoice Amount	Old Plan Payment	Old Plan Balance	New Plan Payment	New Plan Balance
1/15/15			1000		1000
2/1/15	1000	(1000)	1000	(1000) +5% add'l. (50)	950
2/22/15	1250	1000	1250	(1000) + 5% add'l. (50)	1150
3/1/15	1100	1250	1100	(1250) + 5% add'l. (62.50)	937.50

Table 5. Comparison of old payment and new collection system

Key terms

Credit: Not collecting money at the time of sale but giving a specific period of time to pay in the future.

Credit Application: Information about a customer completed on a specific form allowing the company to make credit decisions.

Guarantee: A written agreement with an individual (in the case above) by which collections could be made if the original purchaser does not pay.

References: Companies listed on the credit application which the customer has offered as evidence of their good credit. This list should be called with questions about the customer's history of payment and more.

Terms: The specific amount of time given to pay for goods previously received.

Lesson 5 takeaways

Be Conservative

There isn't much room for error when giving credit. A company could lose money if only a small percentage of customers do not pay. It is difficult to make the correct decisions all of the time, but not giving credit is a safer decision.

One exercise I found to be helpful in catching customers who were turning from a good credit risk to bad was to track the number of days it took to pay every invoice. By tracking the number of days for each invoice a history might reveal a customer is starting to pay slower. For example, after paying every invoice on time, 30 days, the recent history has been between 33 and 37 days. This is a customer with a greater credit risk and should be watched closely.

This is explained and illustrated in the next chapter, but it is most certainly part of the credit issuing process and reiterating this point is not unjustified.

Consider using the chart below when making credit decisions. The pie chart segregates important issues in making credit decisions on importance. It assigns a value to credit information.

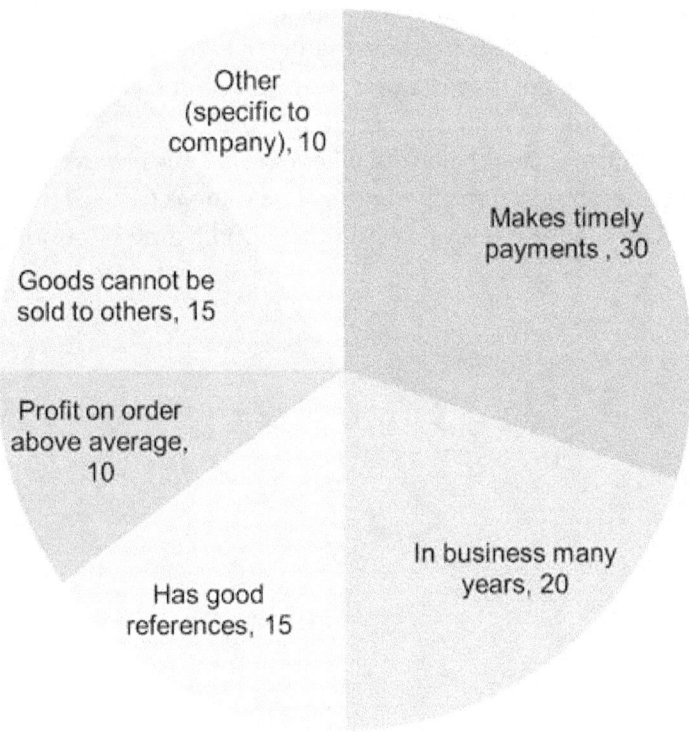

Figure 2. Credit-issuing considerations by percentage of importance

Summary

When it comes to credit, take a few tips from good professional poker players:

- They treat each hand separate and exclusive from any other. Each credit application should be viewed and analyzed separately from any other. Just because one credit application is better than another does not make it good, just better than another.
- If they are unsure of their ability to win a hand, poker players fold their cards. If a credit manager is unsure of issuing credit, then either get more information to become comfortable or fold and decline to issue the credit approval.
- When tired, poker players take a break, get renewed, and come regenerated to fight the battle. The same is true for issuing credit. Only make decisions when in a good frame of mind.

LESSON 6

COLLECTIONS

What is the collection process?

Collections is the process by which a company collects money owed to it from customers who have received credit terms. Customers often purchase product and agree to pay in the future. When the due date comes, the company should have received payment. If a customer does not pay soon after the due date, the company begins the process of collecting the money it is owed.

Why is the collection process so important?

If the collection process is not well-executed, the two most important factors of a business suffer: sales and money (detailed and described earlier).

If a collection person is rude and too forceful when collecting money, the customer might not pay and could refuse to order again.

If a collection person's approach is too meek, it may encourage customers to pay more slowly, taking advantage of a weak collector.

No news is good news?

NOT in this case. Usually no news is good news, but that does not hold true with collections. No check received is bad news.

The fix

There are some very important tasks that might seem mundane at first but can make a big difference between success and failure in the credit and collection aspect of business.

We are creatures of habit

Keep a log of the number of days a customer pays each open invoice. People are creatures of habit, and they often bring their habits into the work place. Checks are printed on Tuesdays and mailed on Wednesdays. The office hours are 9am to 5pm. Lunch is from 1-2pm. Dress attire on Monday through Thursday and jeans and Hawaiian shirts on Fridays. All office supplies come from Staples. Forms to complete for days off, expense reimbursements, vacations, etc. You get the picture. Sometimes this translates to check processing in a company.

What to look for - a break in the consistency of payment

Below is an example of a customer who pays open invoices to a company.

Customer ABCD

Terms: 30 days

Invoice	Invoice Date	Due Date	Invoice Amount	Date Paid	Amount Paid	Balance due	Number days paid after invoice
1256	12/13	1/12	15,000	1/12	15,000	-	30
1458	12/31	1/30	12,500	1/31	12,500	-	31
1756	1/18	2/17	7,500	2/18	7,500	-	31
1956	2/5	3/7	5,500	3/8	5,500	-	31
2156	2/23	3/25	19,500	3/29	19,500	-	34
3305	3/13	4/12	14,500	4/16	14,500	-	34
3745	3/31	4/30	12,750	5/5	12,750	-	35
3966	4/18	5/18	13,750	5/25	13,750	-	37
4105	5/6	6/5	7,500	6/14	7,500	-	39
4855	5/24	6/23	14,000	7/4	10,000	4,000	41

Table 6. Customer invoice payment record

Notice the customer's history of days paid from invoice date. A review of this customer's payments could have predicted a problem, as payments became later and later, resulting in a short payment on the last invoice.

Make visits to customer locations

As each payment is received later than expected, the credit manager should make inquiries with the sales team about any news on the customer; then call the customer. It also may be a good idea to plan a visit to the customer's premises. This is good for both a public relations and an investigative assessment. The visit may reveal empty desks (layoffs) or lack of product on the shelf (in retail cases). Both are signs of a deteriorating business. How many people are working at the customer's location is often an indication of negative changes taking place. Management (often incorrectly) believes the best way to offset bad business is to terminate or lay off staff members.

The credit game

As sure as James Bond will always survive to make another movie, credit given to customers will result in losses due to some who do not pay. It is just the way of the business world.

In my college classes, the issue of credit was discussed in detail. Professors who worked in the business world truly knew their business and were able to make very impressionable lessons. I remembered what they taught and have practiced it throughout my career. (Credit goes to Pace University professors who were excellent in the 70s... the 1970s, not the 1870's.)

Pace University's lessons

The setup: A company has a policy of not offering credit in the marketplace and has revenue of $1 million. The company wants to increase sales, but customers are resistant to increase orders because competitors are offering terms to pay in 30 days. Frustrated, the company tries lowering its prices to induce customers to purchase more from them, but that does not work.

Background: Offering lower prices is often a very dangerous road to take, as it shows customers the company is willing to accept less or may have charged too much in the past. That lower price stays in the memory of customers, who might believe that as long as the product was once offered at a lower price, it will always be available at that price. All they have to do to get the lower price is just be patient. Department stores like Macy's often have sales during the year, and customers know that if they are patient, lower prices will be available. Similarly, Kohl's sends out coupons for 15-30% discounts on all purchases. Most people seem to wait until the sales to shop at Kohl's. (As of this writing, both Macy's and Kohl's are having financial difficulties and closing stores, laying off workers).

What happens: Upon discovering that offering lower prices does not increase revenue, the company wonders if offering credit would increase revenue. The consensus often is that it will (and certainly the sales personnel believe so). Accounting personnel generally raise the flag of doubt. Their doubts include the specter of losses from customers who do not pay, additional personnel needed to work the credit and collection part of the process, cash flow pressures from an increase in revenue (causing the need to purchase more), inventory increases, and many more real concerns. The company decides to return to its existing customers and ask if they would purchase additional amounts if they were issued credit terms. The customer agrees to the additional purchase with credit, and the company ships more goods.

After the long setup of a story, the professor came to the poignant part.

The professor emphatically stated, "The additional sales, called 'marginal sales', are recorded and considered separately from the customer's usual business. Marginal sales have their own Profit and Loss analysis. If the company made $50,000 on marginal sales and collected it entirely, it should issue more credit and take more chances. (The lecture included additional costs of borrowing from a lender to help cash flow and other). The company should continue to issue more and more credit as long as those sales are profitable."

My class, which usually challenged some of the professor's theories, was quiet. It was difficult to argue any point of his lecture, particularly his conclusion. *To repeat, issue more credit, as long as it is profitable.*

How to help gauge results from issuing new credit

Identify responsibility for the project. Often, sales managers and credit managers are at odds over which customers are credit-worthy. One side wins, and the other loses. Let's explore what that means.

- If the goods are shipped over the protest of the credit manager and the customer does not pay, this loss should be on the sales side.
- If the credit manager issues credit and the customer does not pay, it is an accounting loss.
- Points are also awarded when credit decisions turn out right.
- Record all "new" expenses caused by the issuance of credit.
  - From new employees
  - From new administrative costs, like credit agency fees
  - From losses from non-payment
- After a period of time, changes should be made based on the above results as necessary.

How to win the credit game (or at least have a better chance of succeeding)

If a company decides to increase business by 10% by offering credit, it should first do a financial projection of profitability from the increased revenue (marginal sales).

In the example below, an increase of 10% (marginal sales) results in an increase of $ 100,000 in revenue. The company's gross profit is 40%. Estimates of additional costs from credit reports to an additional part-time person and updated computer needs are $ 25,000.

	No Credit	With Credit	Additional Profit (Expense)
Sales	$ 1,000,000	$ 1,100,000	$ 100,000
Cost of goods sold	($ 600,000)	($ 660,000)	($ 60,000)
Gross profit	$ 400,000	$ 440,000	$ 40,000
Overhead	($ 350,000)	($ 375,000)	$ (25,000)
Profit	$ 50,000	$ 65,000	$ 15,000
Bad debts	-	($ 10,000)	($ 10,000)
Profit after bad debts	$ 50,000	$ 55,000	$ 5,000

Table 7. Effect of bad debts on profit and additional profit

Note that if the company projects to increase sales by $ 100,000, it will have a $15,000 profit after expenses. But what if one customer does not pay an invoice of $10,000? The company would still make a $5,000 profit on the marginal sales ($15,000 less the $10,000 bad debt).

The company needs to collect $85,000 ($60,000 for additional Cost of Goods Sold plus $25,000 additional overhead) to break even from the marginal sales. If it collects less than $85,000 of the additional credit it extended ($ 100,000), the company will have lost money.

It might be a good idea to isolate sales from additional credit issued to measure results. Additional sales are viewed as separate from the whole and judged on how much was collected. It might be hard to do because some credit could be given to existing customers with whom the company has experience. With new customers, tracking credit issued is easy; the entire account can be gauged separately.

Companies should monitor the issuance of credit closely and especially when they first begin a new program. Also when getting into the credit side of business, be conservative and plan for contingencies.

Advice from the movies
"If you want peace, plan for War!" XXX from Layer Cake. If you want $ 100,000 of new credit sales, plan for $75,000.

"First part of business, have a plan then stick with it". Frank Martin, The Transporter

This is great advice when offering credit to customers.

What if collections become difficult?

Inevitably, some customers will not pay and others will pay after the due date. The policies a company institutes about collection problems are equally important to its policies when issuing credit.

Few issues are resolved to the satisfaction of the company by threatening a customer and/or legal action. Such a threat should be used sparingly.

More movie advice

Remember Marlon Brando playing the Godfather and James Caan as Sonny? Who achieved more? The Godfather was all about business with no personal challenges to overcome while Sonny only wanted revenge and to enhance his ego, but failed and would have great difficulty replacing the Godfather.

It is the same for collection efforts. The customer has the money, and you don't! How could you get it?

- Egos should be left home. Put away your personal feelings. They do not belong in this arena.
- Understand the problem
- Call the customer and ask what has prevented an on-time payment. Listen and try to find a way to collect the money.

Among the most common responses are:

- Business is bad now, but we believe it will get better soon
- We had a catastrophic loss and are waiting for insurance money to come in
- Our bank is being difficult with us, and we are working to resolve the situation.

As long as you do not hear they are going out of business, your response might be the same.

"HOW CAN WE HELP YOU?"

Really? Is this the best way to respond? Emphatically, YES!

The customer is probably suffering enough, and making demands or threats will not only add to their problems but put you on the "bad" list. Clearly the customer does not have enough money to pay all its bills, so it will probably be making decisions on who to pay and how much. By showing an understanding of their problems, you might make the pay list.

Further, with limited cash and less credit available to them, the customer will have great challenges getting new products. Why not offer to continue to sell them – under your conditions?

Under what conditions

I learned those three very important words early in my career. *Under what conditions.* Most things in life can be accomplished under conditions. War is started or stopped on conditions. Business are purchased and sold under conditions, so why not credit and collections?

The customer is having cash flow issues and cannot pay all its bills.

- Offer to continue selling them on a cash before delivery (CBD) basis. Ask if with each order they can pay an additional amount to cover outstanding balances. Even if they offer 1-2% more than the current invoice, accept it. This is a great idea and helps to collect and make money.
- On new orders, you are getting cash and profits. Even if they do not pay anything extra, think about the profits on the new order as offsetting the losses suffered on their open balance. Do this often enough and profits will cover any bad debts suffered from this account.
- If they ask for some credit, you might consider getting at least your cost plus something extra and take a chance. Ask the customer about their intention for this new order. You might hear

they are expecting to sell to one of their customers and collect quickly. You may offer the customer terms on this order for a very short period (their collection from their customer).

- Another way to overcome a potential bad debt is to put aside the old outstanding amount, creating a new current operating account. Ask the customer if they would like to sign a note (personally guaranteed) for the outstanding amount and pay a monthly amount against the total owed.

  For example, a customer owes $10,000 and agrees to sign a personally guaranteed note. Ask for $ 2,500 as a down payment with the balance, $ 7,500, paid over 18 months or $416.66 per month (plus reasonable interest). Then offer new terms on new orders, shorter and begin with a small amount to see if the customer can adhere to this program. This has worked exceptionally well in certain situations, but be careful not to overextend credit; go slowly. Companies in business many years sometimes hit a bump in the road that can be overcome with time.

Direct collections

There are more ways to collect, but I believe it is crucial to:

- Listen to the issues presently occurring at the customer.
- Determine if the problems are life threatening to the business or not.
- Consider ways to help the customer without losing too much more.
- Make a deal that will benefit both sides, not just one. (Only too often the company is in a position of strength and the customer weak. The company makes demands for payment and terms and the customer is under duress to follow. These types of deals often break down early in the process).
- Maintain consistent communication with the customer not to just collect money but to show interest in how things are going.

Indirect collections

After many years of trying to collect using attorneys, collection agencies and other similar entities, I am exhausted and will do almost anything not to go this route.

Collection agencies

Collection agencies are businesses that make money on turnover. They usually earn their money on a percentage of what they collect. Their interest is solely in collecting money and not the merits of the case. They do not "work" a case but make telephone calls and threaten legal action. Agencies do not focus on any one particular collection unless it is very large. Their methodology is to try to collect money or move to a court proceeding. My success rate with collection agencies has been low.

Collection Lawyers

Collection lawyers are a much better option than are collection agencies. The trick to increasing collectability is to use an attorney local to the client, not the lawyer with whom you play golf. (Often local attorneys are used when your lawyer is not in that vicinity.) My greatest successes have been to go to a local one-man attorney and engage them on a contingency, offering up to 35% of the collection; the more local, the better. Sometimes attorneys can "shame" a customer into paying. They may attend the same church, school board or other community type institutions, so their proximity to the client may be a factor in their collections success.

Case Study 13 – T3 Labs

> *I haven't reported my missing credit card to the police*
> *because whoever stole it is spending less than my wife.*
> *–*ILIE NASTASE

What went wrong - If they won't pay me now, I will wait until they have to

T3 Labs tested a variety of building products, cement, and steel. As a building is constructed, materials used need to be tested, so engineers would visit building sites daily and return to the T3 Labs offices with samples of concrete and other materials to be tested at its laboratories.

A lender called one day to ask if I could perform a bank audit at T3 Labs. As one who rarely, if ever, says no to a bank or a new client, I went up to Ossining, NY, next to Sing-Sing Prison.

T3 Labs had about $ 5 million in accounts receivable, of which approximately $ 3 million was past due over 90 days. Some of the open invoices due from customers were years old.

How can this be?

Questions I needed to ask (besides if there were prison breaks):

1. How were customers allowed to have unpaid invoices for such a long time?
2. Why was the company still doing business with these customers?
3. How could the company survive in business with so much money owed to them?

Answers:

1. Customers received testing services but felt no compelling reason to pay T3 Labs. Only upon completion of the building did the owner **need** to pay T3 Labs and get a C of O (certificate of occupancy) allowing the owner to officially rent to tenants. T3 Labs's management, knowing the building could not open until it gave its approval for a C of O, patiently waited until that time. As long as its lender was willing to advance money for the company to operate, T3 Labs could be patient.

2. If T3 Labs declined new work from these customers, its competitors would get the business. As long as T3 Labs felt it would eventually get its money, the lender would continue to support the company.

3. The lender basically fell asleep and allowed T3 Labs to get "upside-down" and have a loan inconsistent with normal business-banking relationships.

The wake-up call

The lender woke up when T3 Labs's financial picture showed a $ 1.5-million-dollar loss. Not only was the lender worried about collecting current interest payments from T3 Labs, but also concerned about T3 Labs's ability to remain in business.

The fix

After completing the bank audit, I asked the lender for permission to speak with T3 Labs's owner about hiring me to fix some of the problems. He engaged my services, and after 9 months of diligent collection work, the company had decreased its bank loan and improved relations with its lender.

Side note: What I was not able to help was faulty testing by the laboratory that resulted in the owner and many employees getting indicted with some convictions for a variety of reasons. The new Yankee Stadium and the Freedom Tower were buildings cited as having worked with T3 Labs.

How poor collections impact a Company's cash needs

Issuing credit to customers essentially means a company is going to wait for money it might have received at the time of sale, money it could have used to pay employees, vendors, and others. This money could have reduced a bank loan or purchased a special deal from a vendor. Some vendors offer a discount for early payment, and although it may not seem like an attractive deal to make, it is!

How comfortable can a company be that its customers will pay on time? What if they do not pay on time? What are the effects on the business?

The cumulative effect

Let's review each singular issue knowing that a cumulative effect could occur:

Cash flow

A company purchases goods and services on credit and gives a "business" promise to pay within 30 days. The contract between the company and the vendor should be considered sacred to keep the company's reputation in great standing. If this bond is breached, it could lead to disaster for the business.

One vendor claims your company paid late and revokes credit terms given and asks for cash in advance before shipping new goods or providing services. Vendors sometimes talk among themselves and if a company's name comes up in a conversation, it would be great if only good things were said about its ability to pay its invoices on time. One bad apple spoils the barrel, and one vendor who has not been paid on time could tell other vendors who may withdraw credit terms.

Management time

So, how important is the issuance of credit to a company's business health? Very. If your customer does not pay on time, it forces the company to find money elsewhere to pay its vendors. This takes effort on the part of a company's management, time and energy better spent in more productive areas.

Here is an easy way to budget the amount of credit offered to customers and, at the same time, recognize a cash flow problem might occur from outstanding credit.

The accompanying schedule shows if there will be sufficient cash in the bank to pay obligations. The very important part of the schedule is to focus on money due in from customers who have been issued credit.

Example 1 – Good customers pay on time

In the first example, if all customers pay on time, the company will have enough money to pay obligations in a timely manner. The report below is easy to follow if you think about it as your personal check book. You are expecting to get a pay check, deposit it into your bank, then pay what you owe to creditors. A business has this but more deposits and checks.

Accounts Receivable		6/1	6/2	6/3	6/4	6/5
Cash - Starting Balance		500.00	675.00	1,025.00	1,175.00	2,175.00
Money expected to be received from customers						
ABC Company		5,250.00				
Acme Products			1,250.00			
California Frame			3,100.00			
Modern Bus					4,250.00	
Rocket Inc.						3,750.00
Add expected cash from:						
Credit card sales and cash		1,750.00	1,750.00	1,750.00	1,750.00	1,750.00
Total cash expected to be available to pay bills	A	7,500.00	6,775.00	2,775.00	7,175.00	7,675.00
Accounts Payable						
Money due to vendors, others and Payroll						
Battery Place		1,450.00				
Diamond Play		625.00				
Payroll and taxes			4,500.00			
Rent		4,750.00				
Electric			500.00			
Telephone			750.00			
Just in time				1,350.00		
May day				250.00		
Youth co					5,000.00	
	B	6,825.00	5,750.00	1,600.00	5,000.00	-
Cash balance expected	**A - B**	**675.00**	**1,025.00**	**1,175.00**	**2,175.00**	**7,675.00**

Table 8. Cash flow example with on-time paying customers

Example 2 – Customers do NOT pay on time

If customers pay late, as shown in the second example below , the company has no cash to pay bills. And, this is just if the customers pay one day late. It is easy to see if customers pay very late how a truly negative effect would occur.

Accounts Receivable		6/1	6/2	6/3	6/4	6/5
Cash - Starting Balance		500.00	675.00	(3,325.00)	1,175.00	2,175.00
Money expected to be received from customers						
ABC Company		5,250.00				
Acme Products			-	1,250.00		
California Frame			-	3,100.00		
Modern Bus					4,250.00	
Rocket Inc.						3,750.00
Add expected cash from						
Credit card sales and cash		1,750.00	1,750.00	1,750.00	1,750.00	1,750.00
Total cash expected to be available to pay bills	A	7,500.00	2,425.00	2,775.00	7,175.00	7,675.00
Accounts Payable						
Money due to vendors, others and Payroll						
Battery Place		1,450.00				
Diamond Play		625.00				
Payroll and taxes			4,500.00			
Rent		4,750.00				
Electric			500.00			
Telephone			750.00			
Just in time				1,350.00		
May day				250.00		
Youth co					5,000.00	
	B	6,825.00	5,750.00	1,600.00	5,000.00	-
Cash balance expected	A - B	675.00	(3,325.00)	1,175.00	2,175.00	7,675.00

Table 9. Cash flow example with late-paying customers

Of importance to note

The change from example 1 to 2 shows *only two* customers not paying on time (Acme Products and California Frame). The result is a negative

$3,325.00 in the bank on 6/2. Try doing that on a personal account, and the fees charged by the bank for insufficient funds checks could buy a good dinner at a nice restaurant.

Periodic updates

IMPORTANT: This schedule should be updated every day because changes take place every day. Add new collections, invoices to pay, etc. A 2-to-4-week schedule is recommended depending on your company's needs.

Note: The accounts receivable part (cash to be received) will usually have many items in the first date column representing the many customers who pay slowly. This is a very good way for management to review all those past-due customers.

More negative effects from not collecting on time and having less cash

Customer relationships

It often seems almost nonsensical to call a customer who is just a few days past due, but your vendors and the company's reputations rest on this event. Few calls to customers to collect money are good for future business and relationships. Customers are often annoyed by the call and wonder how much difficulty a company is in if you are calling after only a few days of lateness. They may get worried your company is in trouble and look for another supplier.

Banking relationships

Banking relationships are often crucial to a company's survival and growth. If a company shows a wanton respect when issuing credit, its lender may recognize this and become concerned about management's ability to operate successfully and pay its obligations; especially their loans.

Extra efforts of staff

The more credit issued in a company, the more effort is needed to monitor accounts. Newly hired collection persons are eager to have the job and willing to put in the effort to repeatedly call problem accounts. Not so for the second round when collections are finally made and the company sells to that customer again (usually from pressure by the sales team). The difficulty faced in collections usually manifests in a lesser effort by the collections person, who is tired of the event.

Management, who are supposed to monitor collections efforts, may find round one notes will show a diligent effort to collect while round two notes may look like "L/M" for left message. I have found the average life of a collections person in a problematic situation is 6-9 months; they get burned out after that period.

How much credit am I extending?

Extending Credit to Customers

Imagine a customer that purchases $20,000 of products every week and pays at the time of purchase, now requests 30-day payment terms. The company performs a credit check and grants the request. How much extra money does the company need to have on hand? The answer is $80,000.

Week	Invoice	Total Due
1	$20,000	$20,000
2	$20,000	$40,000
3	$20,000	$60,000
4	$20,000	$80,000

Table 10. Covering credit

Replacing the money given as credit

During the 30 days when the customer doesn't pay, the company still has to pay for its purchases, payroll, rent, and everything else. Where does that $80,000 come from? Usually one of two places: the owner puts money into the company or the company takes a loan from the bank. Loans carry interest. That $80,000 may be something closer to $85,000.

This is just for one customer. What size loan would be needed to give credit to every customer? What's the cost for interest? When giving credit terms to customers, you obviously need to make sure that they are worthy of the credit. You also need to be sure that your company can afford it.

We all have been told the large rate of failure of business, especially in their first year of existence. The chart below suggests the rate is quite high.

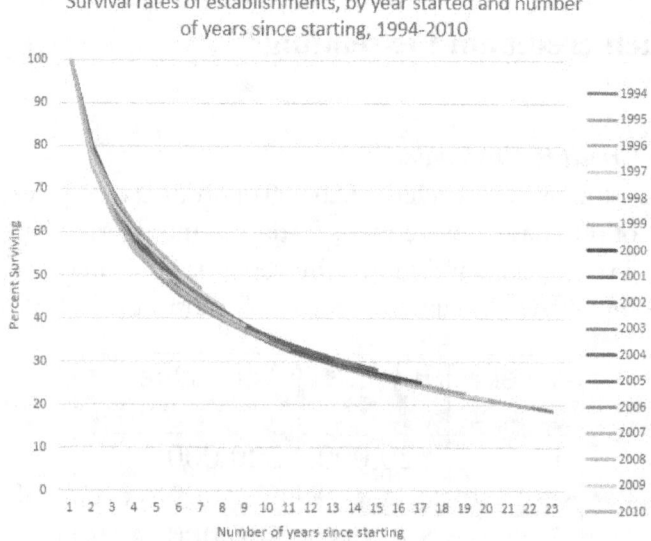

Table 11. Business failure rate

It would be an even more interesting statistic to know the main reasons for failure. Most sources cite the lack of capital, but that is silly since it is impossible to prove a negative. How long would it take for the business to succeed if it had unlimited capital? Maybe never. Since the business ends at some point, it is hard to prove it ever could have succeeded.

I would represent that some business ends because of bad credit policies. Certainly in the first year of business when every dollar counts, any bad debt could hurt a business significantly enough to end its life.

How does a loss affect my future business?

It is easy to both understand and calculate a loss. I offer the following as an example of how losses are much more than just the dollar value loss

Example: A company loses $5,000 because a customer did not pay their open invoice. It is easy to recognize a dollar amount of $ 5,000 was lost, but consider the following question as an alternative way of recognizing a loss: How much in future sales will it take to cover the $5,000 loss? The result could be devastating, as in the example below. The company makes 10% on all sales, so losing $5,000 equates to having to sell $50,000 in new sales to make up for the loss.

	Without losses	With $ 5000 loss
Sales	$ 500,000	$ 50,000
Profit on sales (40%)	$ 200,000	$ 20,000
Overhead (30%)	$ 150,000	$ 15,000
Profit (10%	$ 50,000	$ 5,000

Table 12. What losses actually mean for future business revenue

Key terms

Cash flow: The amount of money needed for the company to fulfill its financial obligations.

Collection efforts: The methodologies used to achieve the objective of collecting from customers.

Marginal sales: The additional amount of sales derived from issuing credit. This is important to gauge along with marginal profits to analyze the value of a program.

Terms: The amount of time a company gave to a customer to pay an outstanding invoice. Remember when giving terms, the customer has both the product/service and your money.

Lesson 6 takeaways

DON'T ENDANGER THE COLLECTION OR ANY CHANCE AT FUTURE BUSINESS WHEN COLLECTING. Consider approaching the situation with respect at the outset. There is no need to begin process with threats or ultimatums; that level can always be implemented.

ALSO, BE VERY CAREFUL ABOUT EXCESSIVE DELAYS offered by customers about payments forthcoming. There is usually only a gut feeling about how long to give before moving to the next phase of collection.

BEFORE EACH COLLECTION CALL OR COMMUNICATION, REVIEW IT often enough to be comfortable the message sent is the one intended. Words can easily be misunderstood. Remember you are only transmitting a message, and it is up to the received to accept your transmission as intended.

Summary

- Plan collections efforts prior to the call
- Understand the financial impact of collections on cash flow
- Have compassion when working on difficult collection calls. Both sides are stressed and it is more likely bad things will occur than good. It takes a cool head and a plan to succeed under these conditions.

LESSON 7

UNDERSTAND BANKING AND BANK LOANS

If you owe the bank $100 that's your problem. If you owe the bank $100 million, that's the bank's problem.
–J. PAUL GETTY

A bank is a place where they lend you an umbrella in fair weather and ask for it back when it begins to rain.
–ROBERT FROST

Borrowing

Many failed businesses end with the line, "The bank shut me down." Banks do not shut down companies that are functioning properly and pay their interest. (They ask the borrower to find another lender at times but do not take over the business to close it down without good cause.)

The most important thing to know from this chapter

There is ONE good reason to borrow money: Future events will allow you to pay it back. Here are two examples. Even in these examples, watch for the problems that can arise.

Event #1 – Waiting for accounts receivable to be collected

The company has sold products on credit to a customer they believe will pay on time. The company needs money to continue operations while waiting for customers to pay. The company can safely borrow money in this situation. However, the caveat is that it only can borrow what it will COLLECT, not what it is owed; companies need to provide for customers who will not pay.

As in the example from the previous chapter, the company issued credit for $80,000 to a customer who had been paying cash at the time of delivery. The customer then asked for credit and the company extended $80,000 to them. The company was now missing this amount from its cash flow for 30 days. It could safely borrow $80,000 from a lender and pay it back when its customer pays off the credit.

A question should be asked if the company needed to borrow $125,000 from a lender. We know why it needs $80,000 but why the extra $45,000? Maybe it is to finance inventory (see below).

Event #2 – Purchasing inventory to resell

The company needs inventory to fill upcoming sales. The company believes it will make a profit on this inventory. Management MUST be aware that unsold or discounted inventory will cost extra money in the form of bank interest (and the economic cost of not having a better product to sell). Borrowing money for inventory that has not yet been sold is a popular way to go out of business, so this must be done with extra consideration.

The company should borrow money to purchase inventory to resell and make profits. It should also make sure the money it borrows is specifically identified as just this (or accounts receivable above) and not to cover business losses.

Case Study 14 - SP Elle

SP Elle is an example of a business that had a built in failure just waiting to happen; like a hand grenade whose pin has been pulled. It is just a matter of time until it explodes. And, its lender was complicit in its demise by continuing to lend money.

SP Elle produced cheap apparel to be sold as "replacement products" to stores. When stores sell out of clothes, it's often hard to replace those same exact products. Retail stores do not want to have empty spaces on the selling floor, so after a good selling product is gone, it needs to be replaced.

SP Elle to the rescue

Much of the apparel we purchase is made overseas and takes a long time to manufacture—so long they would be out of season by the time a new group was completed. When stores sold out of popular clothes, SP Elle would be ready to "replace" goods with similar items. About 75% of SP Elle's sales were from inventory sitting in their warehouse until a store ordered it. Think about puppies at a shelter just waiting for an owner to come, pick them out and take them home. That is how the inventory at SP Elle must have appeared. Stores loved the idea that they could get replacements without having to pre-order.

What went wrong

SP Elle had about $23 million in sales and $5 million in inventory. Much of the inventory was over 2 years old, and some over 5 years old. They also owed about $7 million to the bank. The bank was getting concerned they would never be able to repay the loan. It's easy to see why.

Let's explore one year of business at SP Elle. Their profit margins were low because they were selling to low end stores like Ross and TJ Maxx. They had sales of $23M and spent $16M manufacturing their product. Overhead was about $6.5M. If they sold all of their inventory, their net profit was about $500k. That is a very good year but required all the inventory to be sold.

Because their business model was to sell to low-end stores, it was difficult or impossible to sell their products at a reduced price. If 5% of their inventory went unsold, they would lose money for the year. However, they kept that unsold inventory on the balance sheet at full value, and it looked like they had made a profit, so the bank let them borrow more money.

When the bank recognized what was happening at SP Elle, they changed attitudes about whether SP Elle was a good customer. The company was moved from the regular banking division to the "work-out" section of the bank, where companies go to die. This is the division of the bank where the lending officer tries to recover as much money as possible before pulling the line of credit.

Sport-Elle borrowed money without clearly identifying the reasons it needed money.

Although it borrowed money to finance the manufacture of apparel in hopes of a sale, history clearly showed much of that product would remain in the warehouse, unsold. Using the concept above, it only should have borrowed money that fit one of the two events described: only as much as it took for product it could sell and collect from customers in order to pay its lender. Very soon after its first season, Sport-Elle would have realized it borrowed more than it could pay back (with the difference being the unsold goods on the shelf). And shortly after that recognition, it would have changed its business philosophy or gone out of business

The fix

As usual in business, when there is trouble, some entity is ready to take advantage of the situation - Enter the Factor.

Factoring

If a company wishes to extend credit to its customers and get some money in advance of a customer's payment, factoring may be helpful.

Factoring has become a popular form of lending in today's market, and it differs from traditional lending practices. Factoring is when a loan is based on the company's assets, mainly inventory and accounts receivable.

Here's a simple example in which the company gets to immediately collect money in advance of a sale.

Assume an 80% advance rate for this example:

- The company makes a sale of $100k.
- The factor lends 80% ($80k) and sends that money to the company.
- After 30 days, the customer pays the $100k invoice to the factor.
- The factor sends the remaining $20k, minus their fees, to the company.

The small print

Factoring is an easy concept to understand, but the "small print" makes it tricky in practice. A company must understand the pitfalls or suffer the consequences. Here are some common problems with factoring:

- It's difficult to move from a Factor to a regular bank loan because the company is built around getting immediate income from sales. The company would have to pay the Factor all advances taken and maybe a break-up fee. This total is usually in excess of what a new lender will offer in the form of a new loan. The customer is somewhat stuck with the Factor unless they have money on the sidelines to pay off the Factor.
- Hidden fees. Some factors charge a daily rate to make it hard to see the annual rate is over 15% per annum.
- The Factor controls the relationship. Your business depends on them. If a dispute arises between the company and its customers, the Factor puts its hands over its ears and takes the customer's side until resolution. The amount in dispute becomes ineligible for a loan, and the cash advance from that transaction has to be returned to the Factor.
- Customer complaints, no matter how legitimate, are ineligible for a loan. This gives customers power over a business.
- Late payments from customers also are ineligible for a loan. The factor assumes if the customer has not paid in 90 days, they never will pay and reverses that transaction, asking for the advanced money to be returned.

The key to borrowing money and staying in business

A business pays every day for the privilege of borrowing money. Every time a customer pays late extra money is spent because that money should have been paid to the bank, thereby reducing interest expense.

The best way to borrow money is to consider how that amount will be repaid. If there is a conservative logical plan to repay a loan, take it. If the chance of repaying the loan in a timely manner is suspect, consider alternatives before taking it. Also, calculate the cost of borrowing and include that in the cost of product. Then you'll know whether borrowing is the correct decision.

Key terms

Borrowing: The amount of money a company can pay back from a future business transaction.

Interest: The additional amount of money to be repaid when borrowing. This amount should be used to calculate profits and risk.

Reasons for borrowing: The reason a company needs to borrow money.

Lesson 7 takeaways

Before borrowing money I urge the company to validate the reasons for borrowing. The exercise should begin with the amount of money needed, followed by the business event that will allow the loan to be repaid.

For each loan made, a log should be kept, including the date taken, the reason for the loan, date repaid, and any comments about expectations being met.

Summary

- Loans can help a business to grow in the absence of owners having money to put into the company, but in more cases than not, they are harmful to a business.
- Once taken, loans are hard to repay. My mother always said, "Almost anything is easier to get into than out of." The same is true for a loan.
- If a company finds it is having difficulty repaying a loan, do not hide from the lender. Rather, believe in Nash' equilibrium, which states that all parties should do what is in their best interest. In this case, the lender wants to be repaid and the borrower wants to repay the loan.

LESSON 8

SHIPPING AN ORDER

If you deliver excellence right now, that gives you the
best shot at the best future you've got coming.
—ROBERT FORSTER

I am guessing Mr. Forster did not have business shipments in mind but a personal excellence. Mr. Forster probably did not have to deal with delays in manufacturing.

In most cases, the effort to ship an order is far easier than getting the order. There are generally great barriers to getting an order, including competition, but once taken, only some easier, more mundane tasks remain. Not to diminish the importance and difficulty of administrative and warehousing tasks, but usually there are processes in place that make those tasks easier, especially since they have been done before and often.

From the customer's perspective, once the order has been placed, only the timely delivery of the order matters. The customer has no interest in the manufacturer's problems.

Regardless of the problems and difficulties, companies need to believe the shipping of the order is just as important as making the sale for the order.

Delivery of the order

A felony

In law, there are misdemeanors and felonies. Most of us have watched the *Law and Order* type television programs to know that felonies are more severe crimes than are misdemeanors. Not delivering an order in a timely, efficient, and qualitative manner is a "business" felony. It is hard enough to get an order and make money; it is unconscionable to fall down at the easier part of the sale: the delivery.

In most companies, the emphasis is on getting the order, not the fulfillment of it. After an order is received, the company focuses on the next order. This is a somewhat correct approach but not to the extent of abandoning the manufacturing and shipping part or leaving it to employees only; executives need to be involved in this process.

How does harness racing help to operate a business?

In my younger days, I raced harness horses in mostly amateur races (some professional races as well). Getting a horse to the gate and leaving for position was a strong point of my ability but not the final part of the race: the stretch drive. When the horse and I came into the stretch, I got so excited about winning that my technique fell apart. I had a chance to win. I forgot to keep technically driving on the horse.

A colleague saw me dismayed one day in the driver's changing room and gave me great advice: forget the outcome of the race but concentrate on driving for the mile, after which you can pick your head up to see how you did. Simple and to the point. I took that advice and started to drive much better, getting some wins and the all-important win photo.

I use that same philosophy in business.

After receiving an order (the start of the race), I proceed to the processing of the order (the middle part of the race). The shipping of the order becomes the stretch drive. When all is done properly, the company gets many win photos in the form of future orders and profits.

Insuring the orders go out on time is a very simple process, but that simplicity does not mean all orders will go out perfectly. If something goes wrong, the customers can be alerted prior to the delivery date.

The process

Imagine doing a maze type puzzle, putting a pencil on the start and working toward the end of the maze, which is generally near the middle of the page. Think about putting the pencil at the end of the maze and working back toward the start. It is easier to solve the problem this second way. There are fewer mistakes going down wrong lanes. The shipping process could work in the same manner.

Work backward and assign a time/date to each process

- The order is shipped to the customers (UPS, or truck) - 1 day
- Goods are packed into boxes and labeled for delivery – 1 day
- Order is picked and ready to be checked before packing – 1 day
- Goods are received and placed on warehouse shelves – 2 days
- Manufacturer ships goods – 14 days (from Asia)
- Manufacturing processing time – 4 weeks

To track the process, a working calendar could be created to determine if the order will be manufactured and received in time to ship to the customers.

Here is how it could look on a work-week calendar.

April				
1	2	3	4	5
8 Send order to manufacturer	9	10 Manufacturer begins work	11	12
15	16	17	18	19
22	23	24	25	26 Receive goods from manufacturer
29 Pack goods at warehouse	30 Deliver goods			

Table 13. Backward-scheduled production calendar

Case study 15 – MS Silk (Production)

I worked as a CFO for a convertor whose business was selling fabric to customers in the USA. The goods were designed in the USA but purchased from Japan and Korea. The sale process started with samples shown to customers. After receiving customer orders in the USA, Mayar placed production orders with the factories in Asia.

The customers in the USA wanted to know when the goods would arrive so they could make arrangements for garment sewing. Usual turn-around time was between 60 – 90 days.

What went wrong

Once an order was taken, Mayar went on to designing and selling other fabrics, not worrying about the orders previously taken. Their philosophy relied upon the factory to do its job and get the order done.

The factory would produce the goods and notify Mayar when ready for shipment. Prior to this date, if the goods were late in the manufacturing process, no notice was given. If customers knew in advance of a lateness, they could adjust their schedules for both manufacturing and sale. Contractors (manufacturers) also have schedules, and if a customer's goods are late, they may take another order to manufacture to keep their lines working. Now the customer's order is even later and may cause the retail store to charge a very hefty fee, called a charge back, when goods are delivered late to them.

Often Mayar only knew goods were late when a customer called to inquire about their delivery. Then, Mayar would communicate with the factory, which apologized and advised the order was late. In turn, Mayar alerted the customers about the lateness. Customers were upset with the company for many reasons, all valid. Among them were unnecessarily needing to juggle manufacturing schedules. If they could not get the manufacturer to complete sewing garments in time, they needed to call their customer, the retail store, and ask for more time for delivery. This often came at a cost, whether in dollars or reputation.

The fix

Using the "backward" calendar, I inquired about the manufacturing and shipping process. It was easy to figure out once the schedules and factory protocol were understood.

The Asian factory put the calendar to work and tracked progress through stages like manufacturing, packing, and shipping. This information was readily available from the factory. Mayar could inquire about each step in the process and reconcile that date with the expected delivery date to its customer.

After manufacturing was complete at the factory, a "Go-Down" date was assigned. This was the date the goods were completed and sent to the packing and shipping department. From there, a truck took the goods to a pier to transfer to a boat for shipping. Boats left on Wednesday each week. The boat took about 2 weeks to get to the USA. Mayar's customs broker "cleared" the goods by paying duties and freight and made arrangements for a truck to pick up the goods. The truck then delivered the goods to Mayar's warehouse.

It sounds like a lot to track but therein is the beauty of the "working backward" system's simplicity. If a delivery is to be April 30th, work backwards like in the maze puzzle.

April 30 – Delivery at the Mayar warehouse

April 29 – Arrangements made with trucker to pick up goods at pier for the next day.

April 26 – Customer broker clears the goods by paying duty and freight.

April 10 – Goods need to be on boat (2 weeks from Japan to NYC pier)

Here it got a bit tricky as the boat was schedule for Wednesdays only, so timing centered on the Wednesday day and not a period of time.

April 8 – Goods are finished in Asia and sent to packing and shipping.

Here is how it could look on a five-day workweek calendar:

April				
1	2	3	4	5
8 Goods in packing area	9	10 Goods on boat for delivery USA	11	12
15	16	17	18	19
22	23	24	25	26 Customs broker clears goods
29 Pick up goods at pier	30 Goods scheduled to be at warehouse			

Table 14. Backward-scheduled order tracking calendar

In the communication with the factory each day, Mayar requested an update on orders that were to be completed that week. Occasionally during the daily communications, the office would inquire on the status of orders in process, like this one. Nothing needed to be done if the order was reported to be on schedule.

If the order was reported to be late while in process, a call could be made to the customer advising of such. Any delivery problems could be fixed by shipping the order via air instead of via boat, saving about 10 days in the process.

Side note: the factory in Japan sent packing lists upon shipment showing how many cartons were shipped and the contents of each. What a wonderful opportunity for the company to know this so far in advance.

Take a moment to consider the potential for an extremely efficient system.

Case Study 16 – MS Silk (Shipping)

What went wrong - Two touches

Mayar used the most simplistic system for shipping goods, but it was not the most efficient. All received goods were taken out of the cartons and placed on warehouse shelves. This was touch number one.

After putting all goods on shelves, customer orders were picked for packing and delivery. This was touch number two.

Often, one warehouse person put the goods away and another was sent to pick the order. Another problem was walking around a warehouse picking one order from multiple locations. A person could go from one side of the warehouse to the complete opposite side then back to the original place.

A better system seemed obvious: touch the goods only once before packing and reduce the "steps" necessary to completely pick an order.

The fix

The fix was so easy to understand and implement that it was rejected at first by the warehouse manager because, I believe, it made him seem like a simpleton.

Marry the orders to the goods upon arrival

Knowing goods were in specific cartons allowed Mayar to "marry orders to the cartons. As each carton was opened goods needed to complete and ship customer orders were put into a "staging" area for packing while the balance went to shelves for future shipments.

With the help of the packing list the factory had provided, the warehouse pickers had only to go to the staging area to find the pieces needed instead of going to various shelves in the warehouse to find good for an order. The staging area would contain all goods needed to fill orders. As a bonus for quality control, any pieces remaining in the staging area highlighted the possibility of an error.

Example:

Customer A ordered 1,000 yards each of fabric 123 in blue, red and black. The factory packed all blue fabric in one carton, red in another, and black in another. Prior to changing the system, the warehouse manager would open each carton and put **all** the contents on warehouse shelves before picking orders.

After all the goods were placed on warehouse shelves, customer orders were given to warehouse personnel to pick the goods and bring them to the packing area. The goods would be packed and then shipped to the customer.

Why be inefficient in having to "touch" the goods twice when it all could be done one time? The first touch was to put them on the shelf and the second to pick them for orders.

Software to the rescue

The manufacturer in Asia advised the company when goods were shipped to the USA. Most shipments were sent by boat, which meant a few weeks before arrival in the USA, pickup at the dock, and trucking to the warehouse.

Along with the shipment date came packing slips for specific goods that were shipped. Thus, there was a means for knowing what goods were arriving to fill customer orders. It is no great leap to ask if this data can be used to expedite the shipment of orders. It most certainly can!

The goal was for the computer to highlight which of the receiving goods were needed to fill an existing order. Those goods, when received, should NOT go to the warehouse shelves but be set aside as they will be picked for customer orders. The goods not allocated for customer orders can go to warehouse shelves at a later time (after customer orders have been shipped).

A bit of data entry

A software program (just one) was written that "married" the customer orders to the goods received at the warehouse. Data from the manufacturers packing slip was entered into the new program. Carton 1 – Style 456, color brown, 1,000 yards, Style 234 Green 750 yards, etc.

When all of the goods to be received were entered the computer did its job. It married the goods to be received with customer orders to be shipped.

Printouts would display the item to be picked for an order and the numbered carton it was in.

Order Number 10005			
Style	Color	Yards	Carton
123	Blue	1000	3
123	Red	1000	$8
123	Black	1000	11

Table 15. Packing slip

The warehouse staff began their process by picking customer orders and NOT wasting time putting goods on the shelf. Orders were shipped faster and more efficiently.

One warehouse person was given an order to pick start to finish. For order number 10005, he went to carton number 3 and removed 1,000 yards putting them in an area designated for orders to be completed ("Staging area"). He then went to cartons 8 and 11 and picked the balance of the order. The warehouse manager supervised the process.

Not all goods received were for customer orders, so at the end of the process, unsold goods were checked into inventory and put on shelves.

The "turnaround" of receiving goods and shipping to customers became more efficient.

Case study 17 – CC Creations

We have the orders, but the factory cannot produce the goods
I was hired as the President of CC Creations, a 50-year old intimate apparel manufacturer and wholesaler. Part of the job required my work in factories in Puerto Rico.

What went wrong

The company had over 5,000 pieces ordered by customers but could not ship because the factory could not produce the goods in a timely manner.

The factory was behind in their production schedule by 400 dozen and getting worse. Here is a classic case of a company not being able to deliver orders until long after a promised date. Not only does this delay impair the cash flow of the company (customers pay after goods are received), but also future orders. How can a salesperson sell a second order when the first one has not been shipped?

Fearing arguments about lateness, sales persons reduced calls to customers. Sales persons, in disgust, sent customer calls to the home office for updated shipping information. Eventually, salespersons stopped calling customers altogether and waited for them to call with a reorder. Ugly!

The "fatal embrace"
The main delay in production was due to what is known as a "fatal embrace". This occurs when competing goods need the same machine or process at the same time. Since only one can get the work completed,

the other must wait until the machines are free. In this case, two different styles went to the "boning" area where metal spirals, or bones, were put into the corset. One style went into the production line and was made into a finished product; the other went to a shelf, 7/8 finished, waiting for the machines to become available. Unfortunately for these lonely styles waiting on the shelf, two more competing styles came to boning for completion. The manager called the home office asking which was more important. One went into production and the other to a shelf. The number of garments accumulating on the 7/8 shelf grew disproportionally.

The fix

As easy as the solution to this problem seems to be, it did not happen until the factory manager was asked a question.

"Do you think it might be good to get more workers and machines here?"

His reply was "None of the workers wanted to do this job; it is a hard one."

"How about either offering more money for this job or getting new employees?"

Problem solved.

Is getting an order more important than shipping it? Most definitely yes, but not to the extent poor deliveries affect the company's ability to get new orders.

Key terms

Process: The methodology of completing a customer's order from inception to delivery.

Warehouse efficiency: The manner by which a company reduces the time to pick and ship an order.

Lesson 8 takeaways

As written in Chapter 1 of this book, executives and management should decide what is important to work on and devote enough energy to make it a success. **THE SHIPPING OF ORDERS FALLS INTO THE CATEGORY OF SIGNIFICANT IMPORTANCE.**

Summary

Provide a sentence with a bullet list, as in other lessons.

- Once the paperwork of taking an order has been completed, some of the real work begins – the production and shipping of the order. Few things are harder for a company to understand until customers complain and sales are lost.
- Remember the analogy of driving an entire race. It begins with the start and does NOT end until the finish line has been crossed. The order is taken (start) and timely shipped to customer represents the finish line.

LESSON 9

INVENTORY

There are no secrets to success. It is the result of preparation, hard work, and learning from failure.
—COLIN POWELL

Inventory is product remaining after all orders have been shipped

What is the difference between some inventory and the furniture in your house? Not much. Both do not move often, take up space, and have little resale value.

Each piece of inventory represents a failure to be learned from. This is known because in a perfect world, a business would purchase the exact amount of goods necessary to fill all orders and not one additional piece. Why have extra?

Nothing in business is perfect; errors are made every day. How management reacts to errors measure their success, especially with inventory.

Among the reasons inventory is created include:

- Cancelled customer's orders
- Customers going out of business
- Management over-ordering to get a better price
- Management believing it would sell more than actually accomplished
- And many more

All of this happens on a daily basis, and management needs to do something positive about it.

How to reduce unsold inventory

As humans, we often utilize all the space in basements and attics filling them with stuff we don't use or need at the moment, such as out of season clothes, etc.

Businesses are the same with their summer/winter clothes being excess inventory, old files, and more, but inventory is the real culprit of absorbing space. All inventory businesses seem to have this problem.

Some owners dislike selling anything at a loss because, just maybe, someone will purchase it at a price above cost. Maybe the tooth fairy will leave more than a dollar. They recognize that a loss has occurred, but as long as they do not sell the goods, the loss is not realized. Just words. Like rotting fruit, the value does not increase with time.

Often it is better to sell for whatever price can be achieved. Selling inventory cleans up the warehouse, makes inventory counting easier and, most importantly, brings cash to the table. If the business has a bank loan, money realized from the sale of goods could be used to pay down the principal, thereby reducing the interest due on the loan. A real savings. It also shows the company's lender a good management style.

A secret learned from a genius

I learned something about reducing inventory that no one else (except the person who told me) seems to understand nor practice, yet in its simplicity, it equates to success. It is a solution to resolving losses on inventory and increasing profits. Who would not want to do that? It seems every one of my clients.

Blame me

Note: Early on in my career as a consultant I realized that I was to blame for my clients' errors. Either I did not convince them my way was correct and my ideas should have been implemented, or I did not convince them my way was correct and my ideas should be implemented. Yes, you read the same sentence twice. I needed to be better at my job to convince clients I was correct.

Here was one of the best ideas I learned, practiced my delivery to clients, yet was never able to convince anyone of its merits. So I will again attempt to convince someone of the great benefits of this theory (you, the reader).

Case 16 – JK Natural Fabrics USA

The best way to illustrate my understanding of this philosophy is to return to the days when I was the VP of Finance with JK Natural Fabrics, USA in New York City. The company was a fabric convertor creating the most beautiful designs that were printed on a variety of fabrics for ladies' apparel. The sales process was to make samples for showing to customers in hopes of getting an order.

How much should I order?

Sales persons took orders from customers each day. Management's role was deciding when to place an order with the factory to achieve a timely delivery. If customer orders totaled 19,500 yards, management had to decide if it would place an order with the mill for 20,000 yards or 30,000 yards. Management looked into its crystal ball to decide how many yards to put into work. If 20,000 yards were placed into work, there was less pressure on the sales force to sell the remaining 500 yards unaccounted for in customer orders. The downside of only placing 20,000 yards into work was the limited amount of sales that could be achieved. If 30,000 yards were placed into work, the potential for greater revenue existed but so did additional risk and pressure to sell the balance of production.

One can say it would be a prudent decision to only produce 20,000 yards but under the right circumstances with a strong sales philosophy, the correct move is to produce a higher amount, such as 30,000 yards.

The problem with ordering 10,000 additional yards centers on salespersons who are often looking for the easy sale. They would rather show a customer new product than return to the scene of a sale to offer more yards for sale. This is understood if one subscribes to the successful theory of selling: Once you have made a sale, be quiet. You can only undo the sale. Nevertheless, management wants to increase sales, and one way would be, in this case, to order 30,000 yards.

What if the remaining yards cannot be sold quickly?

The downside of ordering more yardage is revealed should it not be sold quickly. It may not have the "legs" to make the entire race and quit before all yardage is sold. The remaining 10,000 is sold as a "close-out", achieving much less than the original sales price. These are the goods one sees in fabric stores "on sale". One may also see last year's styles in discount stores. Sometimes, the fabrics used to make those garments were purchased as close-outs.

The lesson learned on how to improve on the example above

A co-owner of the company, located in Australia, came to New York to help with operations, advising of a sales approach that had been working very well in Australia.

Salespersons in Australia were instructed to revisit the first customers who purchased yardage to offer more yards for sale at a discount of 5-10%. The sales pitch was that since more yards were ordered than sold (true), the company was offering the excess yards at a discount using the lower prices as an incentive to buy. The customer had calculated the cost of the garment to be made and now could LOWER that cost by purchasing a few yards more at the discounted price. If they intended to make 100 dozen dresses from their original purchase, adding a few more yards to make it 110 dozen dresses might work well for them. The extra 10 dozen dresses could be held for a reorder from their customer or just sold to a new customer.

This is a win-win situation. The fabric supplier sold more yards; the customer sold more garments.

> MORE: The price was reduced gradually over the selling process, creating a seamless sale. Sales managers would scream loudly that it was unconscionable to reduce the price of the goods while in the middle of the selling season. Nevertheless, it was done and to the great success of the company.

The price of the goods was gradually lowered instead of having a precipitous drop off.

This works.

Although this cannot be done in every business, consider it can for many situations in which a product is discontinued or will no longer be carried because of poor performance.

CONCLUSION: get rid of bad inventory as soon as possible.

Unsold Inventory

I have purposefully titled this section unsold inventory to highlight an important fact: all inventory is unsold inventory. If it exists in the warehouse and is not allocated to a specific order, it is inventory, for the following reasons:

- The customer may go out of business between the time the goods are received at the warehouse and the time of shipment to the customer.
- The customer might cancel the order despite having a signed, confirmed purchase order directing shipment. If this is a good customer, it may not pay for the company to fight because of the potential loss of future orders.
- There might have been an error in production or on the sales order, thereby negating the order as one that did not conform to the customer's purchase order.

- Other events could cause a confirmed order not to be shipped and canceled.

The point of naming all goods in the inventory as unsold is specifically to draw attention to a category not presently recognized: an asset/liability.

Accountants view inventory to be an asset. By definition, it is, but that is a financial statement theory, not a practical one. Inventory is an asset on the books and records, carried at its cost. As long as the business can prove inventory has a value greater than cost, it remains an asset at full value on the books. If some part of the inventory becomes old and its value suspect, a determination is made as to how much to "reserve".

I would like to introduce my logic for calling inventory both an asset and liability. The value of the inventory is an asset and should be thought of as having value, but from management's view, here are some reasons to consider the inventory to be a liability:

- If not sold, the cash not generated would
  - NOT Pay down any bank loans thereby reducing interest expense.
  - NOT Pay down any bank loans making the company a more secure risk to the bank.
  - NOT Reduce total bank debt making the company more solvent.
  - NOT be available to Purchase new product, paying cash on delivery and obtaining a purchase discount ($1 - 2\%$ is usual), thereby making the company more money.
- A reduced inventory might lead to a reduced need for warehouse space, consequently saving the company many thousands of dollars in warehouse salaries, rent, utilities, insurance, and other warehousing expenses.
- Physical inventory counts would be easier to conduct with smaller inventories and maybe produce a more reliable inventory.

The above are often called "opportunity" costs, the definition of which centers around "what if" type questions. Again, these are theoretical in nature, and although I agree with that concept, my idea is to truly regard unsold inventory as a detriment to the company.

CONCLUSION: get rid of bad inventory as soon as possible.

Outstanding loans

Most companies have outstanding loans of some type whether the ubiquitous bank loan or extended terms from vendors. Consider how that relationship might change if the bank loan was reduced? How much less interest would be paid? If any significantly detrimental event occurred, how nice would it be to have availability on a bank line to draw funds to cover shortfalls?

CONCLUSION: get rid of bad inventory as soon as possible.

Warehousing costs

It costs money to keep inventory—from extra warehouse personnel to additional space requirements to heat and air conditioning (if lucky).

CONCLUSION: get rid of bad inventory as soon as possible.

Dilemma: two approaches to inventory

Be conservative and order less or be aggressive and order more? Before one can decide, it's important to understand the impact of the choices.

Have enough money to purchase more? I would strongly urge companies to avoid making extraneous purchases if the cash flow does not exist to support the purchase. I truly dislike counting on sales of products to replenish cash flow. It is a very dangerous process. One mistake may adversely affect the company's ability to take advantage of any future price concessions offered by vendors.

Penny wise, pound foolish.

Often product coming from Asia can be delivered via a fast airplane or slow boat. If the company chooses the slow boat, it could take a month or more to get goods. The company might order more than it believes it needs because of the long length of time it takes for delivery. If a product is readily available for delivery, the company might order less each time, keeping its cash available for opportunities.

Miss an opportunity at a bargain?

When I speak of opportunities, bargains or sales are sometimes available to companies with cash or the ability to take additional goods at the right time. Sometimes, manufacturers have unsold inventory, offering it for sale with conditions such as cash on delivery (get a great price if doing this). This is one major reason why a company should not tie up all of its money in unsold inventory. In this case, profits would be lost if the company was not able to purchase at a very low price using available cash.

Have room in the warehouse?

As long as the warehouse can handle additional goods, management may make purchases and have them held for future sale.

How should a company with many items think about its inventory?

Consider a supermarket with the significant number of products carried. The shelves are filled with groceries from canned to packaged, some with shelf lives that are long and others short. Produce has a shorter shelf life than frozen foods and boxed/ packaged goods. How does a supermarket decide what it needs to carry and how much of each item?

Computers today are quite efficient at reporting results from sales. Management knows how many units of a product were sold and for how much money. From that information, new purchases are made. If kumquats are not selling well, they might be replaced by another product.

Managers review every item sold for its contribution to the overall profit of a supermarket. What if a supermarket sold only two canned okra in a month? The projection was that 24 cans would be sold. Among the changes that could be made are to replace this product on the shelf with another one.

Management is looking for a specific gross profit, say 32% (frozen foods), 30% (fruit and vegetables), 30% (meat) and 18% (grocery), respectively. Each of the items in the store is placed into one of these categories. The category is reviewed, and if the gross profit is met a drill-down into specific products may be put on hold pending review of the other categories, but eventually, all items are reviewed (if management is doing their job correctly).

Key terms

Cash flow from the sale of inventory: Money received from the sale of product to be used in the most propitious manner by the company.

Close out: Sale of inventory for less than full price.

Inventory: Product not shipped from the warehouse.

Lesson 9 takeaways

INVENTORY IS ONE THE MOST DANGEROUS AREAS TO A BUSINESS'S SUCCESS. Much time and effort should be made to control it from beginning to end.

BE CAREFUL WHEN PURCHASING. Buy only that which make sense from a sales view. If it can sell for any reasonable amount, buy it. If suspect, think long and hard.

REVIEW CASH FLOW NEEDS of the company when making purchases for the company. Few things deteriorate a company's cash flow faster or more thoroughly than unsold inventory

MUCH THOUGHT NEEDS TO BE GIVEN TO DECIDING ON HOW MUCH INVENTORY TO CARRY because rent and warehouse personnel are very expensive.

"SELL AND REPENT" is my motto. Some can complain about a sale being for a lesser amount than it might have been, but there is little positive to say about a "no" sale.

Summary

- In my practice of helping troubled companies, problem inventory has caused more closures than any other category. One might have guessed a lack of cash was the culprit for business closures. Sure, it probably was, but in many cases the cash shortage was caused by the failure to sell inventory (and/or collect accounts receivable).
- I strongly urge caution when making significant inventory purchases, making sure the company has enough reserves to survive if the purchases cannot be sold as intended.

CONCLUSIONS

A ny one category discussed in the previous lessons can cause disaster if not watched and managed properly. Any combination of problems makes it difficult for management to do their job of managing for progress as they are handling problems.

The solutions to problems are often time consuming and difficult to overcome. Most were not caused in a day, and it seems for every day a problem exists, three are needed to fix it.

The strongest suggestions to overcoming problems are as follows:

- *Touch every aspect of a business every day if possible.* One need not work an entire day collecting past due invoices, but managers should "touch" that topic to see if employees need any help, inquire about past efforts, and tackle the most difficult problems. The same is true for other departments. Management should work with as many employees and departments as possible with the following thought: HOW CAN I HELP THEM GET THEIR JOB DONE?

- *Begin each day studying a cash requirements report.* In many cases knowing how much money will be needed for a specific period of time (4 weeks and 13 weeks, a quarter of the year) will allow management to make better decisions. "We cannot afford to do this now" might change the course of a business from failure to success.

- *Don't be greedy.* This is not to say that quick money cannot be made, but often a deal looks too good to be true because it is just that, not true. Plan for a steady growth and remember the adage that in ten years, three will be good, three bad and four mediocre. Don't believe the good times will last forever; they won't in most cases.

- *Be respectful of your business as a business.* Understand the company may not be a sentient being, but it has a life, a heart, soul, and lungs with which it needs to breathe. Pay it respect by not draining all money (life) out of it for personal reasons.

- *Do not put too much faith in employees who have less of a vested interested in the company than do owners.* They can get other employment but it is much harder to get other businesses. Just look at their resumes to see that fact.

- *Make important decisions under the right circumstances.* If unsure of a decision, hesitate until more facts are known or a clear path is recognized.

- *Study daily "flash" reports of sales, cash, inventory and other important factors of the business.* Look for anomalies that do not make sense— i.e. too much inventory, too little forward customer orders, a low cash balance.

And **good luck**! That is so important to success.

APPENDIX

KEY TERMS

Accounts receivable: Sales made by a company for which the customer did not pay at the time of sale but promises to pay for at a later date.

Bank covenants: Performance restrictions on the lender, contractually agreed to by the borrower, that are reviewed periodically. If not met, penalties (usually financial) are charged.

Borrowing: The amount of money a company can pay back from a future business transaction.

Cash flow: The amount of money needed for the company to fulfill its financial obligations.

Cash flow from the sale of inventory: Money received from the sale of product to be used in the most propitious manner by the company.

Close out: Sale of inventory for less than full price.

Collection efforts: The methodologies used to achieve the objective of collecting from customers.

Commodity business: A business that sells basic items or services like milk, dry cleaning, pizza.

Consumer surplus: The difference between the lowest price a customer has paid for a product and the highest price a customer would be willing to pay for that same product.

Cost of goods sold (COGS): All costs associated with getting a product sold.

Credit: Not collecting money at the time of sale but giving a specific period of time to pay in the future.

Credit application: Information about a customer completed on a specific form allowing the company to make credit decisions.

Gross profit: Revenue minus cost of goods sold.

Guarantee: A written agreement with an individual (in the case above) by which collections could be made if the original purchaser does not pay.

Interest: The additional amount of money to be repaid when borrowing. This amount should be used to calculate profits and risk.

Inventory: Product not shipped from the warehouse.

Marginal sales: The additional amount of sales derived from issuing credit. This is important to gauge along with marginal profits to analyze the value of a program.

Measures of success: Efforts of a business idea reviewed for accomplishments, i.e. money in the bank, new customers, and competent staff. Each category can have its own measure of success.

Overhead: All expenses not related to creating or getting a product to the customer.

Production line scoreboard: Chart listing daily goals versus actual production in a facility.

Projections: A plan created prior to beginning a business to test the likelihood of success.

Also, financial reports that estimate future operations of a business, i.e. cash collections, sales, expenses. The purposes include:

- The creation of a plan that management can accept as practical and sound
- Subsequent review of the plan validating its practicality
- An offering to potential lenders inducing them to make a loan
- And much more.

Process: The methodology of completing a customer's order from inception to delivery.

Reasons for borrowing: The reason a company needs to borrow money.

References: Companies listed on the credit application which the customer has offered as evidence of their good credit. This list should be called with questions about the customer's history of payment and more.

Revenue: Income from product sale.

Seasonal businesses: Businesses whose product is purchased more in one season than another, i.e. ice cream, heating and air conditioning, sun block.

Service schedule: A chart that lists dates for regular equipment maintenance.

Target markets: Segment of the population identified as the most interested in purchasing goods or services from the company.

Terms: The specific amount of time given to pay for goods previously received.

Also, the amount of time a company gave to a customer to pay an outstanding invoice. Remember when giving terms, the customer has both the product/service and your money.

Warehouse efficiency: The manner by which a company reduces the time to pick and ship an order.

LIST OF TABLE AND FIGURES (IN ORDER OF APPEARANCE)

LIST OF CASE STUDIES

Case Study 1 – Gelato Store

How a new business made too many assumptions and over-looked glaring business pitfalls causing it to lose money, close with obligations for the owner that continued after the closure.

Case Study 2 – SP Elle

How a bad business concept was prolonged year after year, causing the company to have significant losses that could not be over-turned in time for their lender to stop loaning money.

Case Study 3 – AAA Books

How a faultily designed business computer program was imple-mented without consideration to profits causing the company to invest in equipment and personnel despite losing more money with each sale.

Case Study 4 – HH Apparel

How a bad sales model was implemented that prevented success even if it succeeded. How a company came to rely on discounts and sale periods for its existence hence encouraging reduced profitability.

Case Study 5 – Torreon, Mexico

How management's lack of attention and care cause products to be incorrectly manufactured.

Case Study 6 – Pco Paper

How a company was not able to correctly calculate the profit made from each sale. If the company knew its costs were actually greater it could have implemented a more profitable sales plan.

Case Study 7 – Moon City Apparel

Another example of a company's inability to calculate the cost of its manufactured product correctly causing them to sell at a lower price than needed to make profits.

Case Study 8 – Steel Convertor

How a lender (bank) can hurt a business' chances of success while making a loan to the business.

Case Study 9 – Costume Jewelry Company

How changes in laws can affect a business and how having a good relationship with a lender can save a business from disaster.

Case Study 10 – California Roofing and Gutter Company

How mismanagement of a business cost the owner the ability to sell it for a large amount of money and retire in luxury.

Case Study 11 – Furniture Store

How issuing credit can not only affect a company's cash flow but also its ability to use that cash for other company operations.

Case Study 12– Pco Paper (2)

How a company issued credit to company's not deserving of it and suffered losses.

Case Study 13 – T3 Labs

How a company allowed its customer to withhold payment of outstanding invoices for years thereby suffering cash shortages covered by extreme bank loans that consequently caused the lender to have great concerns.

Case Study 14 – SP Elle (2)

How inventory is sometimes more or a liability than an asset. How the extreme need to sell inventory is often the difference between success and failure.

Case Study 15 – MS Silk

How a company did not track the production of its goods and consequently did not know if shipments were on time or late. Further, not knowing if goods were late caused problems with customers who were not informed about changes to delivery times.

Case Study 16 - MS Silk (2)

How information was available to make shipping of their product more efficient but ignored. How just a bit of planning could have made the company's shipping faster and more economical.

Case Study 17 – CC Creations

How a factory was operated in a very inefficient manner so as to cause production to severely damage the company's ability to ship existing orders.

Case Study 18 – JK Natural Fabrics

How a company's management CLEARLY understood the need to sell inventory AND make profits simultaneously. BRAVO!

SUGGESTED WORK WEEK

By following the recommendations below, one could effectively control many aspects of a business. The goal of the suggestions below is to provide a checklist of categories that require attention in a business, along with suggestions on what to do to insure all is correctly done.

Here are examples of how I spend my weekends working at my business. Included are the reasons why to perform some tasks on specific days.

One should not think the work week begins on Monday morning. My work week begins on Friday, Saturday and Sunday. I may not physically be in the office on Saturday and Sunday, but I work from my home computer for at least a few hours as preparation days for the work week that begins for employees on Monday. Waiting until Monday to address the needs and issues of a business promotes failure.

On Friday - (Saturday and Sunday)

- Meet with department heads, Shipping, Warehouse, Dispatch, Accounting, etc. Ask each about their plans and needs for the following week. Further, ask what they need to complete their tasks. Your job is to work and support them in achieving their goals.

- It is vital to hit the ground running on Monday morning with a plan.
- Examples of how you could be of help.

1. Warehouse, Shipping, Dispatch - The manager advises an important shipment is expected to arrive at 11am. Some product on this shipment needs to be shipped the same day to an important customer who is expecting a delivery.

Your job could be to call the shipper Monday morning to inquire about the shipment and expected delivery time. If all is on schedule, nothing need be done. If the shipping company says it will be late, 2pm, changes to the plan need to be put into effect. Employees who normally leave at 4pm may be asked to stay late to receive and pick the order. The trucking company who was to have picked up the customer's order at 2pm needs to be called and a later pickup time arranged. Lastly, the customer needs to be called to coordinate a late shipment.

2. Accounting - A wire from a customer was expected on Friday, but it did not appear on the company's bank account. This money is needed to cover the disbursements for the following week. The Controller says they will call the bank on Monday morning for the wire.

If the wire is not received on Monday morning, your job would be to call the customer and inquire about the wire. Sometimes wires get lost in transit, and it takes diligence and persistence to track and redirect to your bank account. Further, if the wire is not forthcoming, arrangements have to be made to obtain other money to cover the missing wire. Being prepared for this on Friday allows you to plan to cordon off time should it be necessary.

3. Sales - The sales staff is prepared to launch the new season's products on Monday, showing them to customers. Samples, price lists, and marketing material have been ordered, received and are in the warehouse.

On Friday, your job would be to insure that each salesperson's package is reviewed to insure all items are included. This will allow an early start to Monday's work. If this is not done and the packages are found to be incomplete on Monday morning, the result would be more administrative and less sales time. Also, a by-product might be a negative attitude for salespersons on a day when they are to be positive sales personnel.

These are only three examples but should be extrapolated into every area of your business.

FOLLOW THE BOY SCOUTS AND BE PREPARED.

RULES OF SUCCESSFUL MANAGERS

I magine the proverbial tiger is chasing you. The tiger represents failure. It is always chasing a business. There is no need to turn around to see how close he is, but assume he is always too close. The way to get separation from the tiger is to follow the rules below.

Rule 1: Touch every part of your business every week.

At some juncture during every week, get involved with all aspects of your business. Work with as many staff members as necessary for them to achieve excellence in performing their jobs. The better they do, the more successful you will be. For employees with whom you do not need intimate discussions and meetings, act interested in them as well. Ask how they are and if they need anything. As innocuous as the question may sound, often it has great meaning to all employees in the company; it shows you care.

Think of the business as your child who needs attention and loving care.

Rule 2: Plan ahead

When so much information is known in advance of an action, planning can help to insure best results. It just requires a bit of attention. Vendor invoices are due at a future date. Shipments from suppliers are scheduled that, in turn, become shipments to customers, accounts receivable, and cash payments. Employee vacations are known in advance.

The job of a manager is to merge all known information to enable better decisions. Of course, there will be bug-a-boos that arise during the week. These issues can be dealt with more effectively by having as much information about the company as possible. The company truck breaks down and needs $15,000 in repairs immediately. Is the money in the checking account? Is there room on the company credit card to charge it? How will this amount be missed from the company's cash flow? What vendor invoices can be paid late without suffering any negative ramifications?

Information is King AND Queen and rules over all provinces.

Rule 3 - Be realistic

Often a manager/owner's personality becomes the culture of the company. Being too positive or negative will often lead to errors, as is normal when polarizing an opinion. Managers should try to avoid too much of either but understand the more realistic they are, the more respect they will earn from employees. If a customer is late in paying an invoice, the unrealistic approach might be for the manager to call the customer and not say, "Don't worry; they will pay."

Your manufacturer calls to say they are running late on your order. Calling them to demand they meet their delivery schedule, or else, is an unrealistic approach to a business problem. Unfortunately, I have experienced too many of my clients using this approach. As time and tide wait for no man, late is late. A realistic approach is to do what is needed to get the shipment as fast as possible. Find out how late the order will be. Ask questions like:

- Are the manufacturer's employees working overtime? Maybe an agreed amount to pay for the overtime might help getting the order done on time. Yes, it is the responsibility of the manufacturer to pay for it, but they may not be willing. A realistic decision needs to be made about the importance of the order to your business.

- When the order is done, can it be shipped faster than the original plan? Maybe an overnight delivery would reduce the lateness. Again, who pays for the enhanced shipping manner is, maybe, irrelevant.

Put your ego aside and do what is best for the business.

Rule 4 - Be a bit paranoid

In life, being a bit paranoid is usually harmful, but in business it has it merits. The operative word is "bit," as too much is harmful but a small amount is very helpful.

Your manufacturer is completing an order for an important customer. They say it will ready by a certain date. A bit of paranoia might suggest a call to insure the manufacturer is on schedule. Doing this and getting a positive answer might help to get a better night's sleep.

Imagine the order is late and on the day of expected delivery, the manufacturer calls to say they will be late. A first question might be to ask when they knew the delivery was going to be late. At this juncture, that question is irrelevant. (You may not trust this manufacturer with future orders, but for now that, also, is a future decision.) Regardless of what caused the lateness, one important fact remains; the company suffers. I believe the company is partially at fault; it is incumbent of the receiver of the order to call the manufacturer to insure a timely delivery. One could argue the manufacturer has the responsibility to call when late, but who suffers? Only the ego is massaged from an argument about who should have called, not the business.

Worry about important events of a business.

Rule 5 - Respect

This category is so important in a business it would take an entire new book to completely cover all respect necessary for success. Examples of how respect makes a successful business include:

a. Your vendors expect to be paid on time. If you do not have money to pay, call as far in advance as you are sure the payment will be late. By sending a late check, you disrespect the relationship with your vendor and endanger future needs from them. The call, despite being a difficult one, will earn respect and trust in most cases.

b. Bankers lend money expecting to have not only the money paid back (with interest) but also an assurance that if something negative is occurring in the company they will be notified. If a law suit is begun against the company, a meeting with the lender to explain the case and its merits is the respectful way to go. If the lender finds out about it from another source, credibility will be lost. The lender now worries about other issues hidden from them, and the lack of respect for this relationship puts the borrower in jeopardy of losing a money source.

c. Employees need a respectful relationship. An owner should not buy a new Mercedes Benz car then tell employees they cannot have a raise because the company is not doing well. Again, this is quite disrespectful and will damage productivity in the company.

After reading the above three examples, I believe the reader can think of many more.

SUGGESTIONS FOR SUCCESS BY CATEGORY

Based upon your company's needs and criteria, here are some suggestions to improve company profits by category.

Cash

1. Complete a bank reconciliation on a daily basis. The information is available on line. This will help to insure your projections are accurate and disclose any unknown charges, i.e. bank interest, automatic payments, etc.

2. While completing the bank reconciliation, notice any checks that have cleared in a 5-7- day period. One of those might be to a valued supplier who is waiting for the check before shipping to you.

3. On Friday, project how much cash you expect to receive in the following week and the amount you expect to disburse. The latter part is easier to determine but knowing how much will be collected is quite a bit harder. It might be hard to believe, but not knowing how much money you will collect is a positive in one respect. It forces a closer attention to accounts receivable, collections, and cash sales.

I often use last year's numbers as a guide, and as each week's cash receipts are plotted and corrected, much can be learned about how to predict this year's more accurately.

Accounts receivable

1. On Friday, as described above, work with the collections department on their plan to collect for the next week.
2. Monday afternoon, after the mail with customer checks has been received. review collection efforts to decide which delinquent accounts you will need to be involved with to collect. Do this on Monday so that any positive effect you might have will be realized in the current week.
3. Report any problem customers to the sales department. Ask the salesperson if they know of anything untoward going on at the company. If not, alert them about the problems and ask if a meeting can be made with the customer. Going with the salesperson somewhat masks the intent of the meeting. The meeting would be to say how valued the customer is and to ask about payment.
4. Review the accounts receivable again on Thursday, working on problem accounts that might need further discussions with the customer or an attorney to help collect.

Inventory

1. Once per week, walk the warehouse with the manager. Discuss all areas of concern and question anything that looks out of place or abnormal. Because the primary objective of a warehouse is to ship goods, other domestic chores are left for a later date to fix. Walking the warehouse with the manager gives both a chance to remark about what needs to get done to insure all goods are neat and available for sale.
2. In a rush to receive and ship goods, sometimes items are put in places "just for the moment", with the intention of putting

them where they belong later. When it comes time to ship the "moment" goods, it takes much time to find them. This is a necessary function in most warehouses. Your job is to be the "reminder".

3. Also during the walk, you can often see items that are not selling. The more you see them on the walks, the greater the understanding about selling them at the best price achievable. (see inventory section again).

Accounts Payable

On Friday (or Saturday/Sunday) review the intended checks to pay vendors. Divide the list into three tiers:

1. Important
2. Need to pay
3. Can wait

This categorization will help in the next week should sufficient cash not be received to pay all.

Employees

1. It is essential to know which employees are scheduled to be out of the office. Your job is to make sure each department missing a person knows and has coverage. This review should be done twice per month.
2. *Walk the floor. This is last and maybe the most important advice I could give. One gets comfortable sitting at a desk working, emailing, calling and getting much done, but more is needed. At least two times per day, walk the entire building and talk to as many employees as possible. Two questions stand out as the most effective:*
   1. How is it going?
   2. What can I do to help you?

Do not expect much when you first start this, but watch the dividends after a short time.

Two times and two questions.

GOOD LUCK!

ABOUT THE AUTHOR

Neil Goldstein has worked in the small business world for over 40 years specializing with troubled companies. After starting as a public accountant, he left for the private world primarily to learn how companies operate in the present time-period. Promotions lead to becoming senior accountants, senior auditors, Controllers, Vice Presidents of Finance and Presidents of companies. In 1996, the desire to help more than just one company at a time was overwhelming, and Neil established a consulting company, Practical Solutions Inc. PSI specialized in helping troubled companies in every aspect of business— from starting a business to obtaining financing. PSI's true calling was helping to prevent companies from closing their doors and filing for bankruptcy. Through the years, PSI expanded, becoming GBI, and presently, Elementary Business Inc. Consulting highlights include formulating a unique plan to help companies avoid bankruptcy, successful factory work in foreign countries, and pride because of the clients who called years after engagements ended to begin new ones or just say thank you for helping them to become successful.

www.ingramcontent.com/pod-product-compliance
Lightning Source LLC
Chambersburg PA
CBHW051702170526
45167CB00002B/500